Residential Care of Children

Fergus Smith
B.Sc.(Hons), M.A., C.Q.S.W., D.M.S., Dip.M

in consultation with
Laura Ritchie
B.A.(Hons), M.Sc, C.Q.S.W.

Children Act Enterprises Ltd
Pantiles Langham Road
Robertsbridge
East Sussex TN32 5EP
tel: 01580 880243

www.caeuk.org

© Fergus Smith 2011

British Library Cataloguing in Publication Data
A catalogue record for this book is available from the
British Library

ISBN 978 1 899986 34 7

Designed and typeset by Helen Joubert Design
Printed in the UK by The Lavenham Press

CAE is an independent organisation which publishes
guides to family and criminal law and provides
consultancy, research, training and independent
investigation services to the public, private and voluntary
sectors.

Contents

Abbreviations

ACA 2002 = Adoption and Children Act 2002
CA 1989 = Children Act 1989
CA 2004 = Children Act 2004
CAFCASS = Children & Families Courts Advisory & Support Service
CSA 2000 = Care Standards Act 2000
CYPA 1969 = Children and Young Persons Act 1969
CYPA 2008 = Children and Young Persons Act 2008
PACE 1984 = Police and Criminal Evidence Act 1984
POCA 1999 = Protection of Children Act 1999

Introduction

- This guide is designed for use by all those in England who provide or work in children's homes (comparable regulations and standards apply to boarding, and residential special schools).

- The guide is intended to facilitate understanding of obligations and expectations of the Care Standards Act 2000 (CSA 2000), Children Act 1989 (CA 1989), other relevant regulations and national minimum standards.

- The Chief Inspector (of Ofsted) will assess, on the basis of the mandatory Children's Homes Regulations 2001 (as amended by the Children's Homes (Amendment) Regulations 2011) and achievement of the national minimum standards (NMS) (issued by the Secretary of State under s.23 (1) CSA 2000 in 2011), whether a children's home should be registered.

- The Chief Inspector may issue a written warning to a service provider which is failing to achieve a required standard. It also has the power to take enforcement action by cancelling registration or initiating a criminal prosecution.

- If the Chief Inspector makes any decision about registration, cancellation, variation or imposition of conditions, it must take into account the national minimum standards and any other factors considered reasonable and relevant.

Definitions (in alphabetical order)

Child

- A person aged less than 18 years old.

Children's Home [s.1 CSA 2000]

- An establishment is a children's home if it provides care and accommodation wholly or mainly for children.

- An establishment is not a children's home:

  - Merely because a child is cared for and accommodated there by a parent/relative or foster carer
  - If it is a health service or independent hospital or clinic, residential family centre, school (but see below) or is of a description excepted by regulation

- A school *is* a children's home if at that time accommodation is provided for children at the school and either:

  - In each of the previous 2 years, accommodation was provided for children at the school or under arrangements made by the proprietor for more than 295 days or
  - It is intended to provide such accommodation for children

Looked After [s.22 CA 1989]

■ A child who is 'looked after by a local authority may be 'accommodated', 'in care' or 'remanded/detained.

■ Accommodation is a voluntary arrangement, the local authority does not gain parental responsibility and no notice is required for removal of the child.

■ In care means that a court has made a child subject of a Care Order which gives the local authority parental responsibility and (some) authority to limit the parents' exercise of their continuing parental responsibility.

■ The local authority has specific authority to detain those who fall into the third category (though with the exception of Emergency Protection Orders, the local authority does not gain parental responsibility), and it may do so as a result of:

  • Remand by a court following criminal charges
  • Detention following arrest by police
  • An Emergency Protection Order or a Child Assessment Order
  • A 'criminal' Supervision Order with a residence requirement

Routes into Residential Care

Accommodating a Child [s.20 CA 1989]

■ One of the family support services the local authority must provide is that of 'accommodating' (in family or residential settings) anyone under 18 'in need' who requires it as a result of:

- There being no person with parental responsibility for her/him
- S/he being lost or having been abandoned or
- The person who has been caring for her/him being prevented temporarily or permanently (for whatever reason) from providing suitable care/accommodation

■ This service is a completely voluntary arrangement and the local authority does not gain parental responsibility.

■ A person with parental responsibility has the right to remove a child from such an arrangement [s.20(8) CA 1989] but:

- A holder of a sole Residence Order could authorise the retention of a child in accommodation in spite of the parent's wishes to remove [s.20(9) CA 1989]
- A young person of 16 or 17 could overrule the parent's wishes to remove her/him [s.20(11) CA 1989]

- Anyone who does not have parental responsibility for a child but does have actual care of her/him may do what is reasonable in the circumstances to safeguard and promote the child's welfare [s.3 (5) CA 1989].

- If 'significant harm' seems likely, emergency protection measures could be used.

Accommodating a 16 or 17 Year Old [s.20 (3) CA 1989]

- A local authority must provide accommodation to a young person in the above age group if:

  - S/he is 'in need' and her/his welfare would otherwise be 'seriously prejudiced'

Accommodating a Young Person Aged 16–20 Years Old [s.20 (5) CA 1989]

- A local authority may provide accommodation in any Community Home which accepts 16+ year olds if it considers it would safeguard or promote the young person's welfare.

Other Obligations To Accommodate [s.21 (1), (2) CA 1989]

- When asked, the local authority must accommodate those:

  - Removed from home on an Emergency Protection Order, Child Assessment Order or an Interim Care Order

- In Police Protection
- Remanded by a court
- Detained under Police & Criminal Evidence Act 1984
- On a Supervision Order with residence requirements [Children & Young Persons Act 1969 [s.12AA]

Local Authority General Duties towards Looked After Children [ss.22, 23, 24 & Sch.2 Children Act 1989 as amended]

All Children

■ Safeguard and promote welfare and make reasonable efforts to allow child access to ordinary services as though still at home.

■ Endeavour, unless not reasonably practical or consistent with welfare, to promote contact between child and:

- Parents, and others with parental responsibility
- Relatives, friends or persons connected with her/him

■ Take reasonable steps to keep parents and those with parental responsibility informed of child's location.

■ Before making any decision, ascertain wishes/feelings of:

- Child
- Parent/s and any others who have parental responsibility and relevant others

■ Give due consideration to these views (having regard in case of child to level of understanding) religion, racial origin, cultural and linguistic background.

NB. A local authority may act in a manner contrary to the above to protect the public from serious injury.

◼ So far as is practical and consistent with welfare, place child with:

- Parents
- Someone who has parental responsibility
- (For a child in care), any previous Residence Order holder
- Relatives or friends or
- Other person connected with her/him

◼ If a child has to be placed with strangers, ensure placement is near home and with any siblings.

◼ Prepare child for leaving looked after status.

◼ The local authority must also take reasonable steps to:

- Reduce criminal/civil proceedings which might lead to Care or Supervision Orders
- Avoid the use of secure accommodation
- Encourage children not to commit crime

Provision of Accommodation & Maintenance for Looked After Children

◼ By virtue of s.8(1) C&YPA 2008, s.23 CA1989 is substituted as follows by:

- *Provision of accommodation for children in care:* when a child is in the care of a local authority, it is its duty to provide her/him with accommodation [s.22A Children Act 1989]

- *Maintenance of looked after children:* it is the duty of a local authority to maintain a child it is looking after in other respects apart from the provision of accommodation [s.22B CA 1989]

■ S.22C *(ways in which looked after children are to be accommodated and maintained)* applies as follows when a local authority is looking after a child C [s.22C (1) CA 1989].

■ The local authority must make arrangements for C to live with a person who falls within s.22C (3) (but subject to s.22C(4)) [s.22C(2) CA1989].

■ A person (P) falls within subsection 22C(3) if:

- P is a parent of C
- P is *not* a parent of C but has parental responsibility for her/him; or
- In a case when C is in the care of the local authority and there was a Residence Order in force with respect her/him immediately before the care order was made, P was a person in whose favour that order was made [s.22C(3) CA1989]

■ S.22C(2) does not require the local authority to make arrangements of the kind mentioned in that subsection if doing so would not be consistent with C's welfare or would not be reasonably practicable [s.22C(4) Children Act 1989].

■ If the local authority is unable to make arrangements under s.22C (2), it must place C in the placement which is, in its opinion, the most appropriate placement available [s.22C(5) CA 1989].

■ In s.22C(5) 'placement' means placement:

- With an individual who is a relative, friend or other person connected with C and who is also a local authority foster parent
- With a local authority foster parent who does not fall within the above category
- In a children's home in respect of which a person is registered under Part 2 Care Standards Act 2000; or
- (Subject to s.22D), placement in accordance with other arrangements which comply with any regulations made for the purposes of s.22 [s.22C(6) CA1989]

■ In determining the most appropriate placement for C, the local authority must, subject to other provisions of this Part (in particular, duties under s.22 CA 1989):

- Give preference to a placement falling within the first paragraph in s.22C(6) above over placements falling within the other 3 paragraphs of that section
- Comply, so far as is reasonably practicable in all the circumstances of C's case, with the requirements of s.22C(8) and

- Comply with s.22C(9) unless that is not reasonably practicable [s.22C(7) CA1989]

- The local authority must ensure the placement is such that:

  - It allows C to live near C's home
  - It does not disrupt C's education or training
  - If C has a sibling for whom the local authority is also providing accommodation, it enables C and the sibling to live together
  - If C is disabled, the accommodation provided is suitable to C's particular needs [s.22C(8) CA 1989]

- The placement must be such that C is provided with accommodation within the local authority's area [s.22C (9) CA 1989].

- The local authority may determine the terms:

  - Of any arrangements its makes under s.22C(2) in relation to C (including terms as to payment); and
  - On which it places C with a local authority foster parent (including as to payment subject to any order made under s.49 CA 2004) [s.22C(10) CA 1989]

  NB. The appropriate national authority may make regulations for, and in connection with, the purposes of s.22 [s.22C (11) Children Act 1989].

- 22D (*review of child's case before making alternative arrangements for accommodation*) provides that:

- When a local authority is providing accommodation for a child (C) other than by arrangements under s.22C(6)(d), it must not make such arrangements for her/him unless it has decided to do so in consequence of a review of C's case carried out in accordance with regulations made under s.26 Children Act 1989

NB. S.22D(1) does not prevent a local authority making arrangements for C under s.22C(6)(d) if it is satisfied that in order to safeguard her/his welfare it is necessary to make such arrangements and to do so as a matter of urgency [s.22D(2).

- 22E *(children's homes provided by appropriate national authority)* provides that:

  - When a local authority place a child it is looking after in a children's home provided, equipped and maintained by an appropriate national authority under s.82(5), it must do so on such terms as that national authority may from time to time determine

- 22F *(regulations as to children looked after by local authorities)* provides that Part 2 of Schedule 2 has effect for the purposes of making further provision as to children looked after by local authorities and in particular as to the regulations which may be made under s.22C(11).

- Schedule 1 (which makes amendments supplementary to, and consequential on, the provisions of s.22 including a power to make regulations about an 'independent review mechanism' for certain decisions in relation to foster parents) has effect [s.8 (2)].

Ensuring Visits to Looked After Children & Others

- S.15 CYPA 2008 introduced a s.23ZA to the Children Act 1989 which applies to a:

  - Child looked after by a local authority
  - A child or young person who was looked after but who has ceased to be looked after by it as a result of prescribed circumstances [s.23ZA(1)]

- It is the duty of the local authority to:

  - Ensure that a person to whom s.23 applies is visited by a 'representative' of the authority
  - Arrange for appropriate advice, support and assistance to be available to a person to whom s.23 applies who seeks it from that local authority [s.23ZA(2) inserted by s.13]

- The duties imposed by s.23ZA(2) are to be discharged in accordance with the *Children Act 1989 (Visits to Former Looked After Children in Detention (England) Regulations 2010* (SI 2797) made for the purposes of this section by the Secretary of State and are subject to any requirement imposed by or under an enactment applicable to the place in which the person to whom this section applies is accommodated (e.g. in custody or detained under the Mental Health Act) [s.23ZA(3)].

■ The regulations (summarised below) make provision about the:

- • Frequency of visits
- • Circumstances in which a person to whom this section applies must be visited by a representative and
- • Functions of a representative [s.23ZA(4)]

■ In choosing a representative a local authority must satisfy itself that the person chosen has the necessary skills and experience to perform the functions of a representative [s.23ZA(5)].

Visits to Former Looked After Children in Detention (England) Regulations 2010

■ The regulations apply to a child (A) who was looked after by a local authority but ceases to be so as a result of being detained pursuant to a court order in a young offender institution (YOI), secure training centre(STC) or a secure children's home [reg.3(1)].

NB. These regulations do not apply to a 'relevant child' as per s.23A Children Act 1989 i.e. one who has already ceased to be looked after.

■ The responsible local authority must ensure that their representative 'R' visits C:

- • Within 10 days of A first being detained, in so far as is reasonably practicable and
- • Thereafter, whenever reasonably requested to do so by A, a member of staff of the institution

where A is detained, any parent of or any other person with parental responsibility for A or the relevant youth offending (YOT) manager [reg.4(1)]

- The responsible local authority may arrange for R to make such additional visits to A having regard to any recommendations made by R in accordance with reg.6(1)(b) [reg.4(2)].

- On each visit R must speak to A in private unless A being of sufficient age and understanding refuses, R considers it inappropriate to do so having regard to A's age and understanding, or R is unable to do so [reg.5].

- R must provide a written report of each visit which must include:

  - R's assessment, having regard to A's wishes and feelings as to whether A's welfare is being adequately safeguarded and promoted whilst in detention
  - R's recommendations as to the timing an frequency of any further visits by R
  - Any other arrangements which R considers should be put in place with a view to promoting contact between A and her/his family or in order to safeguard and promote A's welfare
  - R's assessment as to how A's welfare should be adequately safeguarded and promoted following release from detention in particular whether A will need to be provided with accommodation on

release by the responsible authority or another local authority; whether any other services should be provided by the responsible local authority or another local authority in the exercise of its duties under the Children Act 1989 [reg.6(1)]

■ R's assessment must, unless it is not reasonably practicable to do or it is not consistent with A's welfare take into account the views of:

- Any parent of or any other person with parental responsibility for A
- Appropriate members of staff on the institution in which A is detained [reg.6(2)]

■ The responsible local authority must give a copy of the report to:

- A, unless it would be inappropriate to do so
- Any parent or person with parental responsibility unless to do so would not be in A's best interests
- The governor, director or registered manager of the institution where A is being detained
- The relevant YOT manager
- When different from the responsible local authority, the local authority in whose area A is detained
- Any other person whom the responsible authority considers should be given a copy of the report having regard to R's assessment [reg.6(3)]

■ When making arrangements in accordance with s.23ZA(2)(b) for appropriate advice, support and assistance to be available to A between R's visits, the responsible authority must ensure that:

- The arrangements are appropriate having regard to A's age and understanding, give due consideration to A's religious persuasion, racial origin, cultural and linguistic background and to any disability A may have
- C's wishes and feelings about the arrangements are ascertained and taken into consideration
- As far as is reasonably practicable having regard to A's age and understanding, A knows how to seek appropriate advice, support and assistance from the authority [reg.7]

Additional Duties toward a Child with a Disability

- Work with children who have a disability should be based on the principles that:

  - They are children first and their disability is a secondary, albeit significant issue
  - The aim should be to promote access to the same range of services for all

- Local authorities:

  - Must, so far as is practical, when they provide accommodation for a disabled child, ensure that the accommodation is not unsuitable for her/ needs. [s.23(8) CA 1989]
  - Must maintain, for forward planning purposes, a register of children who have a disability [Sch. 2 para.2 CA 1989]

- May assess a child's needs for the purpose of the Children Act at the same time as any assessment under certain other Acts, e.g. Education Act 1996. Sch.2 para. 3 CA 1989]
- Must provide services for children who have a disability which are designed to minimise the effects of the disability and give them the opportunity to lead as normal lives as possible [Sch.2 para. 6 CA 1989]

- The rights of disabled children to consent to or refuse assessment/treatment or access their records is limited only by the general conditions about sufficient understanding which apply to other children [see CAE's guide to 'Child Protection' for further details].

CARE PLANNING, PLACEMENT & CASE REVIEW (ENGLAND) REGULATIONS 2010

Interpretations & Application of CPP & CR (England) Regulations 2010

- For the purposes of these regulations, the following terms are to be interpreted as described here.

- 'Appropriate person' means:
  - P, if C is to live or lives with P
  - F, if C is to be placed or is placed with F
  - If C is to be placed, or is placed in a children's home, the person registered under Part 2 Care Standards Act 2000 as carrying on or managing the home
  - If C is placed or to be placed in accordance with other arrangements under s.22C(6)(d), the person who will be responsible for C at the accommodation on behalf of the responsible authority (if any)

- 'Area authority' means the local authority for the area in which C is placed or to be placed, if this is different from the responsible authority

- 'C' means a child who is 'looked after' by the responsible authority

- 'Care plan' means the plan for the future care of C prepared in accordance with regs.4–8 of these regulations.

- 'Case record' has the meaning given in reg.49 (see p.85).

■ 'Connected person' means a relative (grandparent, brother, sister, uncle or aunt – of full or half blood, or by marriage/civil partnership or step-parent), friend or other person connected with C.

■ Director of Children's Services means the officer of the responsible authority appointed for purposes of s.18 Children Act 2004.

■ 'F' means a person who is approved as a local authority foster parent and with whom it is proposed to place C, or as the case may, C is placed.

■ 'Health plan' means the arrangements made by the responsible authority to meet C's health care needs.

■ 'Independent visitor' means the person appointed to be C's visitor under s.23ZB Children Act 1989 and reg.47.

■ 'IRO' means the independent reviewing officer appointed for C's case under s.25A(1); the 'officer' means the director children's services or other senior officer of the responsible authority nominated in writing by the director to act on behalf of her/him.

■ 'P' means:

- A person who is C's parent
- A person who is not C's parent but who has gained parental responsibility for C or
- If C is in the care of the responsible authority and there was a Residence Order in force for C immediately before the Care Order was made, a person in whose favour that order was made

■ 'Pathway plan' has the meaning of s.23E Children Act 1989 i.e. a plan setting out for:

- 'Eligible children', the advice, assistance and support which the local authority intends to provide while it is looking after the person and later (including when s/he may cease to be looked after) and
- 'Relevant children', the advice, assistance and support the local authority intends to provide under Part III Children Act 1989

■ 'Personal adviser' means the personal adviser arranged for C under para.19C Sch.2.

■ 'Personal education plan' means the arrangements made by the responsible authority to meet C's educational and training needs.

■ 'Placement' means the arrangements made by the responsible authority to provide for C's accommodation and maintenance by any of the means specified in s.22C Children Act 1989.

■ 'Placement plan' – see reg.9(1) page.32

■ 'R' means the representative of the responsible authority who visits C in accordance with arrangements made by it under s.23ZA Children Act 1989.

■ The 'responsible authority means the local authority that looks after C.

- 'Working day' means any day other than a Saturday or Sunday, Christmas day or Good Friday or a bank holiday in England and Wales.

Arrangements for Looking After a Child

Care Planning [Reg.4 CPP&CR (England) Regulations 2010]

▪ If a child (C) is not in the care of the responsible authority and a care plan for her/him has not already been prepared, the responsible authority must assess C's needs for its services to achieve or maintain a reasonable standard of health or development, and prepare such a plan [reg.4(1)].

▪ Except in the case of a child to whom s.31A applies (i.e. one subject to Care Proceedings in which case the court will set the time within which the care plan must be prepared), the care plan must be prepared before C is first placed by the responsible authority or, if it is not practicable to do so, within 10 working days of the start of the first placement [reg.4(2)].

NB. If C was first placed by the responsible authority before 01.04.11, the care plan must be prepared as soon as reasonably practicable [reg.4(6)]

▪ When assessing C's needs under para.1, the responsible authority must consider whether the accommodation provided for C meets the requirements of Part 3 of the 1989 Act i.e. will enable the discharge of all the duties in Part 3 [reg.4(3)].

■ Unless reg.4(5) applies the care plan should so far as is reasonably practicable be agreed by the responsible authority with:

- Any parent of C's and any person who is not C's parent but who has parental responsibility for her/him, or
- If there is no such person, the person who was caring for C immediately before the responsible authority arranged a placement for C [reg.4(4)]

■ If C is aged 16 or over and agrees to be provided with accommodation under s.20(1) CA 1989 as amended, the care plan should be agreed with C by the responsible authority [reg.4(5)].

Preparation & Content of Care Plan [Regs.5, 6 & Sch. 1 CPP&CR (England) Regulations 2010]

■ The care plan must include a record of the following:

- Long term plan for C's upbringing ('the plan for permanence')
- Arrangements made by the responsible authority to meet C's needs in relation to health (inc. information set out in para. 1 Sch.1 of these regulations (the 'health plan', see below) education and training, inc. information in para.2 of Sch.1 (the 'personal education plan', see below); emotional and behavioural development, identity, with particular regard to C's religious persuasion, racial origin and cultural and linguistic background, family and social

relationships and in particular the information set out in para.3 of Sch.1(see below); social presentation, and self-care skills

- Except in a case when C is in the care of the responsible authority but is not provided with accommodation by it by any of the means referred to in s.22C, the placement plan
- Name of the independent reviewing officer (IRO)
- Details of the wishes and feelings of the persons listed in s.22(4) about the 'arrangements' referred to above, the placement plan that have been ascertained and considered in accordance with s.22(4) and (5) and the wishes and feelings of those persons in relation to any change, or proposed change, to the care plan [reg.5].

◼ The responsible authority must keep C's care plan under review in accordance with Part 6 of these regulations (Case Reviews) and, if it is of the opinion some change is required, they must revise the plan or make a new plan accordingly [reg. 6(1)].

◼ Unless otherwise allowed by these regulations, the responsible authority must not make any significant change to the care plan unless the proposed change has first been considered at a review of C's case [reg.6(2)].

◼ The responsible authority must give a copy of the care plan to:

- C, unless it would not be appropriate to do so having regard to her/his age and understanding

- P
- The IRO
- If C is to be placed, or is placed with F, the fostering service provider that approved F in accordance with the Fostering Services Regulations
- If C is to be placed, or is placed in a children's home, to the person registered under Part 2 Care Standards Act 2000 in respect of that home
- If C is to be placed, or is placed, in accordance with other arrangements under s.22C(6)(d), to the person who will be responsible for C at the accommodation [reg.6(3)]

■ The responsible authority may decide not to give a copy of the care plan, or a full copy of the care plan to P if to do so would put C at risk of significant harm [reg.6(4)].

Information to be Included in the Health Plan [Sch.1 para.1 in Support of Reg.5 CPP&CR (England) Regulations 2010]

■ C's state of health including physical, emotional and mental health [Sch.1 para.1(1)].

■ C's health history including, as far as practicable, C's family's health history [Sch.1.para.1(2)].

■ The effect of C's health and health history on C's development [Sch.1 para.1(3)].

■ Existing arrangements for C's medical and dental care, appropriate to C's needs, including:

- Routine checks of C's general state of health, including dental health
- Treatment and monitoring for identified health (including physical, emotional and mental health) or dental care needs
- Preventive measures such as vaccination and immunisation
- Screening for defects of vision or hearing; and
- Advice and guidance on promoting health and effective personal care [Sch.1 para.1(4)]

■ Any planned changes to the arrangements [Sch.1 para.1(5)]

■ The role of the appropriate person, and of any other person who cares for C, in promoting C's health [Sch.1.para.1(6)]

Information to be included in the Personal Education Plan [Sch.1 para.2 in Support of Reg.5 CPP&CR (England) Regulations 2010]

■ C's educational and training history including information about educational institutions attended and C's attendance and conduct record; academic and other achievements; and C's special educational needs, if any [Sch.1 para.2(1)].

■ Existing arrangements for C's education and training including details of any special educational provision and any other provision made to meet C's particular educational or training needs and to promote C's educational achievement [Sch.1 para.2(2)].

- Any planned change to existing arrangements for C's education or training and if any changes are necessary, provision made to minimise disruption to that education or training achievement [Sch.1 para.2(3)].

- C's leisure interests [Sch.1 para.2(4)].

- The role of the appropriate person and of any other person who cares for C in promoting C's educational achievements and leisure interests [Sch.1 para.2(5)].

Family & Social Relationships [Sch.1 para.3 in Support of Reg.5 CPP&CR (England) Regulations 2010]

- If C has a sibling for whom the responsible authority or another authority is providing accommodation and the children have not been placed together the arrangements made to promote contact between the, so far as is consistent with C's welfare [Sch.1 para.3(1)].

- If C is looked after by, but is not in the care of, the responsible authority details of any order relating to C made under s.8 [Sch.1 para.3(2)].

- If C is a child in the care of the responsible authority, details of any order relating to C made under s.34 (parental contact etc with children in care) [Sch.1 para. 3(3)].

- Any other arrangements made to promote and maintain contact in accordance with para.15 of Sch.2

so far as is reasonably practicable and consistent with C's welfare between C and any parent of her/him; any person who is not a parent but has parental responsibility for C and any other connected persons [Sch.1 para.3(4)]

■ If s.23ZB(1) (appointment of independent visitor) applies, the arrangements made to appoint an independent visitor for C, or if s.23ZB(6) applies (appointment of independent visitor not made when child objects) that fact [Sch.1. para.3(5)].

Health Care [Reg.7 CPP&CR (England) Regulations 2010]

■ Before C is first placed by it, or if that is not reasonably practicable before the first review of C's case the responsible authority must make arrangements for a registered medical practitioner to:

- Carry out an assessment of C's state of health
- Provide a written report of the assessment, addressing the matters specified in para.1 of Sch.1 to these regulations (i.e. the health plan, see above) as soon as reasonably practicable [reg.7(1)]

■ Reg. 7(1) does not apply if in the 3 months immediately preceding placement, an assessment of C's state of health has been carried out and the responsible authority has obtained a written report that meets the requirements of that paragraph [reg.7(2)].

- The responsible authority must make arrangements for a registered medical practitioner or a registered nurse or registered midwife acting under the supervision of a registered medical practitioner, to review C's state of health and provide a written report of each review, addressing the matters specified in the 'health plan' at least every:

  - 6 months before C's 5th birthday, and
  - 12 months after C's 5th birthday [reg.7(3)]

- Reg.7(1) and (3) do not apply if C refuses consent to the assessment, being of sufficient understanding to do so [reg.7(4)].

- The responsible authority must take all reasonable steps to ensure that C is provided with appropriate health care services, in accordance with the health plan, including:

  - Medical and dental care and treatment, and
  - Advice and guidance on health, personal care and health promotion issues [reg.7(5)]

Contact with a Child in Care [Reg.8 CPP&CR (England) Regulations 2010]

- Reg. 8 applies if C is in the care of the responsible authority and the responsible authority has decided under s.34(6) CA 1989 (refusal of contact as a matter of urgency) to refuse to allow contact that would otherwise be required by virtue of s.34(1) or an order under s.34 (parental contact etc with a child in care) [reg.8(1)].

■ The responsible authority must immediately send written notification to the following persons of the information specified in reg.8(3) below:

- C, unless it would not be appropriate to do so having regard to C's age and understanding
- P
- If, immediately before the Care Order was made a person had care of C by virtue of an order made in exercise of the High Court's inherent jurisdiction with respect to children, that person
- Any other person whose wishes and feelings the responsible authority consider to be relevant, and
- The IRO [reg.8(2)]

■ The information specified in reg.8(2) above is:

- The responsible authority's decision
- Date of the decision
- Reasons for the decision
- Duration of the decision (if applicable), and
- Remedies available in case of dissatisfaction [reg.8(3)]

■ The responsible authority may depart from the terms of any order made under s.34 CA 1989 by agreement with the person in relation to whom the order is made, provided that:

- C, being of sufficient understanding, also agrees, and
- Written notification of the specified information is sent within 5 working days to the persons specified in reg.8(2) [reg.8(4)]

- If the responsible authority has decided to vary or suspend any arrangement made (otherwise than under an order under s.34) with a view to affording any person contact with C, it must immediately give written notification containing the specified information to the persons listed in reg.8(2) [reg.8(5)]

- The responsible authority must record any decision made under this regulation in C's care plan [reg.8(6)].

Placements: General Provisions

Placements Plan [Reg.9 & Sch. 2 CPP&CR (England) Regulations 2010]

■ Subject to reg.9(2) or (4), before making arrangements in accordance with s.22C for C's accommodation the responsible authority must:

- Prepare a plan for the placement ('the placement plan') that sets out how the placement will contribute to meeting C's needs, and
- Includes all the matters specified in Sch.2 (reproduced below) as are applicable, having regard to the nature of the placement and
- Ensure that C's wishes and feelings have been ascertained and given due consideration and that the IRO has been informed [reg.9(1)] (see page 21)

■ If it is not reasonably practicable to make the placement plan before making the placement, it must be made within 5 working days thereafter [reg.9(2)].

■ The placement plan must be agreed with, and signed by, the appropriate person [reg.9 (3)].

NB. If the arrangements for C's placement were made before 01.04.11, the responsible authority must prepare the placement plan as soon as reasonably practicable [reg.9(4)].

Particulars that Must be Included in C's Placement Plan [Sch.2 CPP&CR (England) Regulations 2010]

■ How on a day to day basis C will be cared for and her/his welfare safeguarded and promoted by the appropriate person [Sch.2 para.1 (1)].

■ Any arrangements made for contact between C and any parent of C's and any person who is not C's parent but who has parental responsibility for C, and between C and other connected persons inc. if appropriate, the reasons why contact with any such person would not be reasonably practicable or would not be consistent with C's welfare; if C is not the care of the responsible authority, details of any order made under s.8;, if C is in the care of the responsible authority, details of any order relating to C made under s.34 (parental contact etc with children in care); the arrangements for notifying any changes in contact arrangements [Sch.2 para.1(2)].

■ The arrangements made for C's health (including physical, emotional and mental health) and dental care including the name and address of C's registered medical and dental practitioners and, where applicable, any registered medical or dental practitioner with whom C is to be registered following the placement; any arrangements for delegation and exercise of responsibility for consent to medical or dental examination or treatment for C [Sch.2 para.1(3)].

■ The arrangements made for C's education and training inc. the name and address of any school at which C is a registered pupil and the name of the designated teacher at that school (if applicable); the name and address of any other education institution that C attends or of any other person who provides C with education or training; if C has a statement of special educational needs, details of the local education authority that maintains the statement [Sch.2 para.1(4)].

■ The arrangements made for R to visit C in accordance with Part 5 (visits by the responsible authority's representative etc), the frequency of visits and the arrangements made for advice support and assistance to be available to C between visits in accordance with reg.31 (advice, support and assistance for the child) [Sch.2 para.1(5)].

■ If an independent visitor is appointed, the arrangements made for them to visit C [Sch.2 para.1(6)].

■ The circumstances in which the placement may be terminated and C removed from the appropriate person's care in accordance with reg.14 [Sch.2 para.1(7)].

■ The name and contact details of:

- The IRO
- C's independent visitor (if one is appointed)
- R and

- If C is an 'eligible child', the personal adviser appointed for C [Sch.2 para.1(8)]

■ Additional information to be included if C is placed with P:

- Details of support and services to be provided to P during the placement [Sch.2 para. 2(1)]
- The obligation on P to notify the responsible authority of any relevant change in circumstances, including any intention to change address, any changes in the household in which C lives, and any serious occurrence involving C [Sch.2 para.2(2)]
- The obligation to ensure that any information relating to C or C's family or any other person given in confidence to P in connection with the placement is kept confidential and that such information is not disclosed to any person without the consent of the responsible authority [Sch.2 para.2(3)]
- The circumstances in which it is necessary to obtain in advance the approval of the responsible authority for C to live in a household other than P's household [Sch. 2 para.2(4)]
- The arrangements for requesting a change to the agreement [Sch.2 para.2(5)]
- The circumstances in which the placement will be terminated in accordance with regulation 19(c) (ii) (child placed with parents etc before assessment completed) [Sch.2 para.2(6)]

◼ Additional information to be included if C is placed with F, in a children's home or in other arrangements:

- The type of accommodation to be provided, its address and, when C is placed in other arrangements under s.22C(6)(d), the name of the person who will be responsible for C at that accommodation on behalf of the responsible authority (if any) [Sch.2 para.3(1)]
- C's personal history, religious persuasion, cultural and linguistic background, and racial origin [Sch.2 para.3(2)]
- If C is looked after but is not in the care of the responsible authority – the respective responsibilities of the responsible authority and C's parents or any person who is not C's parent but who has parental responsibility for C; any delegation of responsibility to the responsible authority there has been for C's day to day care there has been by C's parents or any person who is not C's parent but has parental responsibility for C; the expected duration of the arrangements and the steps which should be taken to bring the arrangements to an end, inc. arrangements for C to return to live with C's parents or any person who is not C's parent but who has parental responsibility for C; and if C is aged 16 or over and agrees to being provided with accommodation under s.20, that fact [Sch.2 para.3(3)]
- Any circumstances in which F must obtain the prior approval of either the responsible authority

or P before making decisions in relation to C or C's care [Sch.2 para.3(4) as amended]

- The responsible authority's arrangements for the financial support of C during the placement [Sch.2 para.3(5)]
- If C is placed with F, the obligation on F to comply with the terms of the foster care agreement made under reg.27(5)(b) of the Fostering Services (England) Regulations 2011 [Sch.2 para. 3(6)]

Avoidance of Disruption in Education [Reg.10 CPP&CR (England) Regulations 2010]

- Subject to reg.10 (2) and (3), if C is a registered pupil at a school in the 4th key stage, a decision to make any change to her/his placement that would have the effect of disrupting the arrangements made for C's education must not be put into effect until it has been approved by a 'nominated officer' [reg.10(1)].

- Before approving a decision under reg.10(1), the nominated officer must first be satisfied that:

  - C's wishes and feelings have been ascertained, and given due consideration
  - The educational provision made for C at the placement will promote her/his educational achievement and is consistent with C's personal education plan
  - The designated teacher at the school had been consulted and
  - The IRO had been consulted [reg.10(2)]

NB. The 'designated teacher' for a maintained school is the member of staff designated by the governing body in accordance with s.20 (1) CYPA 2008. Academies, City Technology Colleges and City Colleges for the Technology of the Arts are required by their funding arrangements to have a designated teacher. The Designated Teacher (Looked After Pupils etc) (England) Regulations 2009 SI 2009/1538 prescribe the qualifications and experience of the designated teacher.

■ Reg.10(1) does not apply in any case when the responsible authority terminates C's placement in accordance with reg.14(3) (termination of placements) or it is necessary for any other reason to change C's placement and in such a case the responsible authority must make appropriate arrangements to promote C's educational achievement as soon as reasonably practicable [reg.10(3)].

■ In any case not falling within reg.10(1), but where the responsible authority propose making any change to C's placement that would have the effect of disrupting the arrangements made for C's education or training, the responsible authority must ensure that other arrangements are made for C's education or training that meets C's needs and are consistent with C's personal education plan [reg.10(4)].

NB. In this regulation '4th key stage' means a pupil in the 4th stage for purposes of Part 6 or 7 of the Education Act 2002; 'registered pupil' has the meaning given in s.20(7) Children and Young Persons Act 2008 and 'school' has the meaning given in s.4 Education Act 1996 (i.e. an educational institution outside further and higher educations sectors for providing primary and/or secondary education) [reg.10(5)].

Placements out of Area [Regs.11–12 CPP&CR (England) Regulations 2010]

■ Subject to regs.11(3) and 11(4), a decision to place C outside the area of the responsible authority (including a placement outside England) must not be put into effect until it has been approved by a nominated officer [reg.11(1)].

■ Before approving a decision under reg.11(1), the nominated officer must be satisfied that:

- C's wishes and feelings have been ascertained and given due consideration
- The placement is the most appropriate placement available for C and consistent with her/his care plan
- C's relatives have been consulted where appropriate
- The area authority had been notified
- The IRO has been consulted [reg.11(2)]

■ In the case of a placement made in an emergency reg.11(2) does not apply and before approving a decision under reg.11(1), the nominated officer must:

- Be satisfied that C's wishes and feelings have been ascertained and given due consideration and that the placement is the most appropriate placement available for C and consistent with her/his care plan
- Take steps to ensure that the IRO is informed, relatives consulted and area authority notified within 5 working days of the approval of the decision under reg.11(1) [reg.11(3)]

- Reg.11(1) and (2) do not apply to a decision to place C outside the area of the responsible authority:

  - With F who is a 'connected person'
  - With F who is approved as a local authority foster parent by the responsible authority

- Reg. 12 applies if C is in the care of the responsible authority, and the responsible authority makes arrangements to place her/him outside England and Wales in accordance with the provisions of para.19 of Sch.2 (placement of a child in care outside England and Wales) [reg.12(1)].

- The responsible authority must take steps to ensure that, so far as is reasonably practicable, requirements corresponding with the requirements which would have applied under these regulations had C been placed in England, are complied with [reg.12(2)].

- The responsible authority must include in the care plan details of the arrangements made to supervise C's placement [reg.12(3)].

Notifications of Placements [Reg.13 CPP&CR (England) Regulations 2010]

- Subject to reg.13(3), the responsible authority must give written notice to the persons listed in reg.13(2) below of the arrangements for C's placement before the placement is made or, if immediate placement is necessary, within 5 working days after the placement is made, unless it is not reasonably practicable to do so [reg.13(1)].

- The persons referred to in reg.13(1) are:

  - C, unless it would not be appropriate to do so having regard to C's age and understanding
  - Any parent of C's and any person who is not C's parent but who has parental responsibility for C (or if C is in the care of the responsible authority and there was a Residence Order in force on C immediately before the Care Order was made, a person in whose favour the Residence Order was made)
  - If C is in the care of the responsible authority, any person who is allowed contact with C under s.34(1) CA 1989 and any person who has contact with C by virtue of an order under s.34 of that Act (contact with a child in care by parents etc)
  - If C is looked after, but is *not* in the care of the responsible authority, any person who has contact with C pursuant to an order made under s.8 (Residence, Contact and other orders with respect to children)

- Any person who was caring for C immediately before the arrangements were made
- The Primary Care Trust (or in the case of a child living or to be placed in Wales, the local Health Board) for the area in which C is living and, if different, for the area in which C is to be placed,
- C's registered medical practitioner and, when applicable, the registered medical practitioner with whom C is to be registered during the placement
- Any educational institution attended by, or person providing education or training for, C, and
- The IRO [reg.13(2)]

▣ The responsible authority may decide not to give notice to any or all of the persons listed in roundels 2–4 above if to do so would place C at risk of significant harm [reg.13(3)].

Termination of Placement by the Responsible Authority [Reg.14 CPP&CR (England) Regulations 2010]

▣ Subject to regs.14(3) and 14(5) the responsible authority may only terminate C's placement following a review of C's case in accordance with Part 6 of these regulations [reg.14 (1)].

▣ Subject to reg.14(3), before terminating C's placement, the responsible authority must:

- Make other arrangements for C's accommodation, in accordance with s.22C

- Inform the IRO
- So far as is reasonably practicable, give written notice of its intention to terminate it to all the persons to whom notice of the placement was given under reg.13; the person who is providing the placement; if C is placed in the area of another local authority, the area authority [reg.14(2)]

■ If there is an immediate risk of significant harm to C or to protect others from serious injury, the responsible authority must terminate C's placement and in those circumstances:

- Reg.14(1) does not apply
- The responsible authority must make other arrangements for C's accommodation, in accordance with s.22C and inform the IRO as soon as reasonably practicable [reg.14(3)]

■ If it is not reasonably practicable to notify any person in accordance with reg.14(2) then the responsible authority must give written notice to that person within 10 working days of the placement's termination [reg.14(4)].

■ Regulation 14 dos not apply if C's placement is terminated under reg.19(c), reg.23(2) or reg.25(6) nor if s.22D (review of child's case before making alternative arrangements for accommodation) applies [reg.14(5)].

Provision for Different Types of Placement: Placement of a Child in Care with Parents etc

Application [Reg.15 CPP&CR (England) Regulations 2010]

■ Regs.15–21 apply if C is in the care of the responsible authority and it, acting in accordance with s.22C(2), proposes to place C with P [reg.15(1)].

NB. Nothing in regs. 15–21 requires the responsible authority to remove C from P's care if C is living with P before a placement decision is made about her/him [reg.15(2)].

Effect of Contact Order [Reg.16 CPP&CR (England) Regulations 2010]

■ The responsible authority must not place C with P if to do so would be incompatible with any order made by the court under s.34 Children Act 1989 (parental contact with children in care etc) [reg.16].

Assessment of P's Suitability to Care for a Child [Reg.17 & Sch.3 CPP&CR (England) Regulations 2010]

■ Before deciding to place C with P, the responsible authority must:

- Assess the suitability of P to care for C inc. the suitability of the proposed accommodation and all other persons aged 18 and over who are members of the household
- Take into account all the matters set out in Sch.3 (reproduced below) in making its assessment
- Consider whether, in all the circumstances and taking into account the services to be provided by the responsible authority, the placement will safeguard and promote C's welfare and meet C's needs set out in the care plan and
- Review C's case in accordance with Part 6 [reg.17]

Matters to be Taken into Account When Assessing Suitability of P to Care for C [Sch.3 CPP&CR (England) Regulations 2010]

- P's capacity to care for children and in particular in relation to C to:
  - Provide for C's physical needs and appropriate medical and dental care
  - Protect C adequately from harm or danger, and from any person who presents a risk of harm to C
  - Ensure that the home environment is safe for C
  - Ensure that C's emotional needs are met and C is provided with a positive sense of self, including any particular needs arising from C's religious persuasion, racial origin and cultural and linguistic background, and any disability C may have

- Promote C's learning and intellectual development through encouragement, cognitive stimulation and the promotion of educational success and social opportunities
- Enable C to regulate C's emotions and behaviour, including by modelling appropriate behaviour and interactions with others; and
- Provide a stable family environment to enable C to develop and maintain secure attachments to P and other persons who care for C

- P's state of health including P's physical and mental and emotional health and medical history including any current or past issues of domestic violence, substance misuse and mental health problems.

- P's family relationships and composition of P's household, including particulars of:

  - Identity of all other members of the household, including their age and the nature of their relationship with P and with each other, including any sexual relationship
  - Any relationship with any person who is a parent of C
  - Other adults not being members of the household who are likely to have regular contact with C, and
  - Any current or previous domestic violence between members of the household, including P

- P's family history, including particulars of:

- P's childhood and upbringing including the strengths and difficulties of P's parents or other persons who cared for P
- P's relationships with P's parents and siblings, and their relationships with each other
- P's educational achievement and of any specific learning difficulty or disability, and
- Chronology of significant life events, and
- Particulars of other relatives and their relationships with C and P

■ Particulars of any criminal offences of which P has been convicted or in respect of which P has been cautioned.

■ P's past and present employment and other sources of income.

■ The nature of the neighbourhood in which P's home is situated and resources available in the community to support C and P [Sch.3 para.1]

■ In respect of members of the household aged 18 and over, so far as is practicable, all the particulars specified above should be taken into account except those relating to P's family history, her/his past and present employment and the nature of the neighbourhood in which P's home is situated [Sch.3 para.2].

Decision to Place a Child with Parent (P) etc [Reg.18 CPP&CR (England) Regulations 2010]

■ The decision to place C with P must not be put into effect until it has been approved by a nominated officer and the responsible authority has prepared a placement plan for C [reg.18(1)].

■ Before approving a decision under reg.18(1), the nominated officer must be satisfied that:

- • C's wishes and feelings have been ascertained and given due consideration
- • The requirements of reg.17 (suitability) have been complied with
- • The placement will safeguard and promote C's welfare
- • The IRO has been consulted [reg.18(2)]

Circumstances in which a Child May be Placed with a Parent (P) Before Assessment Completed [Reg.19 CPP&CR (England) Regulations 2010]

■ If the nominated officer considers it to be necessary and consistent with C's welfare, the responsible authority may place C with P before its assessment under reg.17 ('the assessment') is completed, provided that it:

- • Arranges for P to be interviewed in order to obtain as much of the information specified in Sch.3 (see above) about P and the other persons living in P's household who are aged 18 and over as can be readily ascertained at that interview

- Ensures that the assessment and review of C's case are completed in accordance with reg.17 within 10 working days of C being placed with P and
- Ensures that a decision in accordance with reg.18 is made and approved within 10 working days after the assessment is completed and if the decision is to confirm the placement, review the placement plan and, if appropriate amend it; and if the placement is not so confirmed, terminate it [reg.19]

Support for Parents etc [Reg.20 CPP&CR (England) Regulations 2010]

■ If C is placed or to be placed with P, the responsible authority must provide such services and support to P as appear to it to be necessary so as to safeguard and promote C's welfare and must record details of such services and support in C's care plan [reg.20].

Provision for Different Types of Placement: Placement with Local Authority Foster Parents

Interpretation [Reg.21 CPP&CR (England) Regulations 2010]

- For the purposes of regs.21–26 'registered person' is defined in s.2(1) Fostering Services Regulations 2011.

- If C is placed jointly with 2 persons each of whom is approved as a local authority foster parent, any reference in these regulations to a local authority foster parent is to be interpreted as referring equally to both such persons and any requirement to be satisfied by or relating to a particular local authority foster parent must be satisfied by, or treated as relating to, both such persons [reg.21(2)].

Conditions to be Complied with Before Placing a Child with a Local Authority Foster Parent [Reg.22 CPP&CR (England) Regulations 2010]

- Reg. 22 applies when the responsible authority proposes to place C with F [reg.22(1)].

- The responsible authority may only place C with F if:

  - F is approved by the responsible authority, or provided that the conditions specified in reg.22 (3) are also satisfied, another fostering service provider

- The terms of F's approval are consistent with the proposed placement, and
- F has entered into a foster care agreement either with the responsible authority or with another fostering service provider in accordance with reg. 27(5)(b) of the Fostering Services Regulations 2011 [reg.22(2)]

- The conditions referred to above are that:

  - The fostering service provider by whom F is approved consents to the placement
  - Any other local authority which has placed a child with F consents to the placement [reg.22(3)]

Emergency Placement with a Local Authority Foster Parent [Reg.23 CPP&CR (England) Regulations 2010]

- If it is necessary to place C in an emergency, the responsible authority may place C with any local authority foster parent who has been approved in accordance with the Fostering Services Regulations, even if the terms of that person's approval are not consistent with the placement provided that the placements is for longer than 6 working days [reg.23(1)].

- When the period of 6 working days referred to above has expired, the responsible authority must terminate the placements unless the terms of that person's approval have been amended to be consistent with the placement [reg.23(2)].

Temporary Approval of a Relative, Friend or Other Person Connected with C [Reg.24 & Sch. 4 CPP&CR (England) Regulations 2010]

■ If the responsible authority is satisfied that the most appropriate placement for C is with a connected person, even though s/he is not approved as a local authority foster carer, and that it is necessary for C to be placed there before that person's suitability to be a local authority foster carer has been assessed in accordance with the Fostering Services Regulations, it may approve that person as a local authority foster parent for a temporary period not exceeding 16 weeks ('temporary approval') provided that it first:

- Assesses the suitability of the connected person to care for C, including the suitability of the proposed accommodation, and all other persons aged 18 and over who are members of the household in which it is proposed that C will live
- When making its assessment, takes into account the matters set out in Sch.4 of these regulations reproduced below (assessment of suitability of a connected person to care for C),
- Consider whether, in all the circumstances and taking into account the services to be provided by the responsible authority, the proposed arrangements will safeguard and promote C's

welfare and meet C's needs identified in the care plan, and

- Make immediate arrangements for the connected person's suitability to be a local authority foster parent to be assessed in accordance with the Fostering Services Regulations ('the full approval process') before the period of temporary approval expires [reg.24(1);(2)].

NB. In reg.24, 'connected person' means a relative, friend or other person connected with C [reg.24(3)].

Matters to be Taken into Account When Assessing Suitability of a Connected Person to Care for C [Sch.4 CPP&CR (England) Regulations 2010 in support of Reg.24]

■ In respect of the connected person:

- The nature and quality of any existing relationship with C

■ Her/his capacity to care for children and in particular in relation to C:

- Provide for C's physical needs and appropriate medical and dental care
- Protect C adequately from harm or danger including from any person who presents a risk of harm to C
- Ensure that the accommodation and home environment is suitable with regard to the age and developmental stage of the child
- Promote the learning and development of C

- Provide a stable family environment which will promote secure attachments for C, including the promotion of positive contact with P and other connected persons unless to do so is not consistent with the duty to safeguard and promote C's welfare

- Her/his state of health, including physical, emotional and mental health and medical history including any current or past issues of domestic violence, substance misuse or mental health problems.

- Family relationships and composition of her/his household including particulars of:

  - Identity of all other members of the household inc. their age and nature of their relationship with the connected person and each other, inc. any sexual relationship
  - Any relationship between C and other members of the household
  - Other adults not being members of the household who are likely to have regular contact with C and
  - Any current or previous domestic violence between members of the household inc. the connected person

- Their family history inc:

  - Particulars of their childhood and upbringing including strengths and difficulties of their parents or other persons who care for them

- Their relationships with their parents and siblings and relationships with each other
- Their educational achievement and any specific learning difficulty or disability
- A chronology of life events
- Particulars of other relatives and their relationship with C and the connected person

■ Particulars of any criminal offences of which they have been convicted or in respect of which cautioned.

■ Past and present employment and other sources of income.

■ The nature of the community in which their home is situated and resources available in the community to support C and the connected person.

Expiry of Temporary Approval [Reg.25 CPP&CR (England) Regulations 2010]

■ Subject to reg.25(4), the responsible authority may extend the period of temporary approval of a connected person if either:

- It is likely to expire before the full approval process is completed, or
- The connected person, having undergone the full approval process, is *not* approved and seeks a review of the decision in accordance with regulations made under para.12F(1)(b) of Sch.2 CA 1989 (independent review mechanism) [reg.25(1)]

■ In a case when the temporary approval is likely to expire before the full approval process is completed, the responsible authority may extend the period of temporary approval once for a further period of up to 8 weeks [reg.25(2)].

■ In a case when a person is not approved and is seeking a review of that decision, the responsible authority may extend the period of temporary approval until the outcome of the review is known [reg.25(3)].

■ In either case, before deciding whether to extend the temporary approval the responsible authority must first:

- Consider whether placement with the connected person is still the most appropriate placement available
- Seek the views of the fostering panel established by the fostering service provider in accordance with the Fostering Services Regulations, and
- Inform the IRO [reg.25(4)]

■ A decision to extend temporary approval must be made by a nominated officer [reg.25(5)].

■ If the period of temporary approval and of any extension to that period expires and the connected person has not been approved as a local authority foster parent in accordance with the 2002 Regulations, the responsible authority must terminate the placement after first making other arrangements for C's accommodation [reg.25(6)].

Independent Fostering Agencies – Discharge of Authority Functions [Reg.26 CPP&CR (England) Regulations 2010]

- An authority may make arrangements in accordance with reg.26 for the duties imposed on it by reg.14(3) (termination) and reg.22 (conditions to be complied with before placing a child with a local authority foster parent) to be discharged on its behalf by a registered person [reg.26(1)].

- No arrangements may be made under reg.26 unless the responsible authority has entered into a written agreement with the registered person which includes the information (reproduced below) set out in para.1 of Sch.5 of these regulations, and when the responsible authority proposes to make an arrangement under reg.26 in relation to a particular child, the written agreement must also include the matters set out in para.2 of Sch.5 [reg.26(2)].

- The responsible authority must report to the Chief Inspector of Education Children's Services and Skills any concerns it may have about the services provided by a registered person [reg.26(3)].

Agreement with an Independent Fostering Agency (IFA) Relating to the Discharge of the Responsible Authority's Functions [Sch.5 CPP&CR (England) Regulations 2010 in support of Reg.26]

- The agreement must contain the following information:

- Services to be provided to the responsible authority by the registered person
- Arrangements for the selection by the responsible authority of F from those approved by the registered person
- A requirement for the registered person to submit reports to the responsible authority on any placements as may be required by the responsible authority and
- Arrangements for the termination of the agreement [Sch.5 para.(1)]

- If the agreement relates to a particular child, it must also contain the following information:

  - F's details
  - Details of any services that C is to receive and whether the services are to be provided by the responsible authority or by the registered provider
  - Terms (including as to payment) of the proposed placement agreement
  - Arrangements for record keeping about C and for the return of records at the end of the placement
  - A requirement for the registered person to notify the responsible authority immediately in the event of concerns about the placement and
  - Whether and on what basis other children may be placed with F [Sch.5 para. (2)]

Provision for Different Types of Placement: Other Arrangements

General Duties of the Responsible Authority When Placing a Child in other Arrangements [Reg.27 & Sch. 6 CPP&CR (England) Regulations 2010]

- Before placing C in accommodation in an unregulated setting under s.22C(6)(d) ('other arrangements'), the responsible authority must:

    - Be satisfied that the accommodation is suitable for C having regard to the matters set out in Sch. 6 to these regulations (reproduced below)
    - Unless it is not reasonably practicable arrange for C to visit the accommodation, and
    - Inform the IRO

Matters to be Considered before Placing C in Accommodation in an Unregulated Setting under s.22C(6)(d) Children Act 1989 [Sch.6 CPP&CR (England) Regulations 2010 in support of Reg.27]

- In respect of the accommodation:

    - Facilities and services provided
    - State of repair
    - Safety
    - Location
    - Support
    - Tenancy status

- Financial commitment involved for C and their affordability [Sch.6 para.1]

■ In respect of C, C's:

  - Views about the accommodation
  - Understanding of their rights and responsibilities in relation to the accommodation
  - Understanding of funding arrangements [Sch.6 para.2]

Visits by Responsible Authority's Representative etc

Frequency of Visits [Reg.28 CPP&CR (England) Regulations 2010]

- As part of its arrangements for supervising C's welfare, the responsible authority must ensure that its representative ('R') visits C wherever C is living in accordance with reg. 28 [reg.28(1)].

- Subject to regs.28(3)–(6), the responsible authority must ensure that R visits C:

  - Within 1 week of the start of any placement
  - At intervals of not more than 6 weeks for the first year of any placement and thereafter
  - If the placements is intended to last until C is 18, at intervals of not more than 3 months and in any other case intervals of not more than 6 weeks [reg.28(2)]

- When reg.19 applies i.e.' circumstances in which a child may be placed with P before assessment completed', the responsible authority must ensure that R visits C:

  - At least once a week until the first review carried out in accordance with Part 6 and
  - Thereafter at interval of not more than 6 weeks [reg.28(3)]

■ When reg.24 applies i.e. 'temporary approval of relative, friend or other person connected with C', or an interim Care Order has been made in relation to C under s.38 and C is living with P, the responsible authority must ensure that R visits C:

- At least once a week until the first review carried out in accordance with Part 6
- Thereafter at intervals of not more than 4 weeks [reg.28(4)]
- If a Care Order has been made in relation to C under s.31 (Care and Supervision Orders), and C is living with P, the responsible authority must ensure that R visits C:
- Within 1 week of the making of the Care Order
- Thereafter at intervals of not more than 6 weeks [s.28(5)]

■ If C is in the care of the responsible authority but another person is responsible for the arrangements under which C is living for the time being ('C's living arrangements'), the responsible authority must ensure that R visits C:

- Within 1 week of the start of C's living arrangements and within 1 week of any change to C's living arrangements
- At intervals of not more than 6 weeks for the first year thereafter
- At intervals of not more than 3 months in any subsequent year [reg.28(6)]

- In addition to visits in accordance with reg.28(2)–(6) the responsible authority must ensure that R visits C:

  - Whenever reasonably requested to do so by C; if C is provided with accommodation by the responsible authority, the appropriate person; or if C is in the care of the responsible authority but another person is responsible for her/his living arrangements, *that* person
  - Within 1 week of first receiving notification under s.30A Care Standards Act 2000 (notification of matters relating to persons carrying on or managing certain establishments or agencies), when the children's home in which C is placed for the time being is referred to in the notification [reg.28(7)]

Conduct of Visit [Reg.29 CPP&CR (England) Regulations 2010]

- On each visit, R must speak to C in private unless:

  - C, being of sufficient age and understanding to do so, refuses
  - R considers it inappropriate to do so, having regard to C's age and understanding, or
  - R is unable to do so [reg.29]

Consequences of Visits [Reg.30 CPP&CR Regulations (England) 2010]

- If as a result of a visit carried out in accordance with the above regulations, R's assessment is that C's welfare is not adequately safeguarded and promoted by the placement, the responsible authority must review C's case in accordance with Part 6 [reg.30]

Advice, Support & Assistance for the Child [Reg.31 CPP&CR (England) Regulations 2010]

■ When making arrangements in accordance with s.23ZB(2)(b) for advice, support and assistance to be available to C between R's visits, the responsible authority must ensure that:

- The arrangements are appropriate having regard to C's age and understanding, and give due consideration to C's religious persuasion, racial origin, cultural and linguistic background and to any disability C may have
- So far as is reasonably practicable having regard to C's age and understanding, C knows how to seek appropriate advice, support and assistance from them [reg.31]

Reviews of the Child's Case

General Duty of the Responsible Authority to Review the Child's Case [Reg.32 CPP&CR (England) Regulations 2010]

- The responsible authority must review C's case in accordance with these regulations [reg.32(1)].

- The responsible authority must not make any significant change to C's care plan unless the proposed change has first been considered at a review of C's case, unless this is not reasonably practicable [reg.32(2)].

- Nothing in these regulations prevents any review of C's case being carried out at the same time as any other review assessment or consideration of C's case under any other provision [reg.32(3)].

Timing of Reviews [Reg.33 CPP&CR (England) Regulations 2010]

- The responsible authority must first review C's case within 20 working days of the date on which C becomes looked after [reg.33(1)].

- The second review must be carried out no more than 3 months after the first, and subsequent reviews must be carried out at intervals of no more than 6 months [reg.33(2)].

- The responsible authority must carry out a review before the time specified in reg.33(1) or (2) if:

- The IRO so requests
- Reg.30 (consequences of R's report) applies
- C is provided with accommodation under s. 21(2)(b) or (c) (i.e. detained under PACE 1984, remanded or subject of a Supervision Order with a residence requirement) and a review would not otherwise occur before C's ceases to be so provided with accommodation
- C is in care the care of the authority and, is detained in a secure training centre (STC), or a young offenders institution (YOI) and a review would not otherwise occur before C ceases to be so detained or
- C is looked after but is *not* in the care of the responsible authority, the responsible authority propose to cease to provide accommodation for C, and accommodation will not subsequently be provided for C by C's parents or any person who is not C's parent but who has parental responsibility for C [reg.33(3)]

Conduct of the Review [Reg.34 CPP&CR (England) Regulations 2010]

■ The responsible authority must have a policy regarding the manner in which it will review C's case and provide a copy to C (unless not appropriate having regard to age and understanding), C's parents or any person who is not C's parent but who has parental responsibility for C, and any other person whose views the responsible authority consider to be relevant [reg.34(1);(2)].

■ The considerations to which the responsible authority must have regard in reviewing each case are set out in Sch.7 to these regulations, reproduced below.

For Consideration at Each Review [Sch.7 in Support of Reg.35 CPP&CR (England) Regulations 2010]

■ The effect of any change in C's circumstances since the last review, in particular of any change made by the responsible authority to her/his care plan and whether decisions taken at the last review have been successfully implemented, and if not the reasons for that.

■ Whether the responsible authority should seek any change in C's legal status.

■ Whether there is a plan for permanence for C.

■ The arrangements for contact and whether there is any need for changes to the arrangements in order to promote contact between C and P, or other connected persons.

■ Whether C's placement continues to be the most appropriate available, having regard to the reports of R's visits to C, and whether any change to the placement plan or any other aspects of the arrangements made to provide C with accommodation is, or is likely to become necessary or desirable before the next review of C's case.

■ C's educational needs, progress and development and whether any change to the arrangements for C's education and training is, or is likely to become, necessary or desirable to meet C's particular needs and to promote C's educational achievement before the next review of C's case, having regard to the advice of any person who provides C with education or training, in particular the designated teacher of any school at which C is a registered pupil.

■ C's leisure interests.

■ The report of the most recent assessment of C's state of health obtained in accordance with reg.8 and whether any change to the arrangements for C's health care is, or is likely to become, necessary or desirable before the next review of her/his case, having regard to the advice of any health care professional received since the date of that report, in particular C's registered medical practitioner.

■ Whether C's needs related to C's identity are being met and whether any particular change is required, having regard to C's religious persuasion, racial origin and cultural background.

■ Whether the arrangements made in accordance with reg.31 (advice support and assistance for the child) continue to be appropriate and understood by C.

■ Whether any arrangements need to be made for the time when C will no longer be looked after by the responsible authority.

- C's wishes and feelings, and the views of the IRO, about any aspect of the case and in particular about any changes the responsible authority has made since the last review or proposes to make to the C's care plan.

- If reg.28(3) applies (visiting obligations in C is placed with P before reg.17 assessment completed), the frequency of R's visits [Sch.7].

Role of the IRO [Reg.36 CPP&CR (England) Regulations 2010]

- The IRO must:

  - So far as reasonably practicable, attend any meeting held as part of the review ('the review meeting') and, if attending the review meeting, chair it
  - Speak to C in private about the matters to be considered at the review unless C, being of sufficient understanding to do so, refuses or the IRO considers it inappropriate having regard to C's age and understanding
  - Ensure that so far as reasonably practicable, the wishes and feelings of C's parents or any person who is not C's parent but has parental responsibility for C, have been ascertained and taken into account
  - Ensure the review is conducted in accordance with Part 6 and in particular that the persons responsible for implementing any decision taken in consequence of the review are identified, and

that any failure to review the case in accordance with Part 6 or to take proper steps to implement decisions taken in consequence of the review are brought to the attention of an officer at an appropriate level of seniority within the responsible authority [reg.36(1)]

- The IRO may, if not satisfied that sufficient information has been provided by the responsible authority to enable proper consideration of any of the matters in Sch.7 (reproduced above), adjourn the review meeting once for not more than 20 working days, and no proposal considered in the course of the review may be implemented until the review has been completed [reg.36(2)].

Arrangements for Implementing Decisions Arising out of Reviews [Reg.37 CPP&CR (England) Regulations 2010]

- The responsible authority must:
  - Make arrangements to implement decisions made in the course, or as a result, of the review, and
  - Inform the IRO of any significant failure to make such arrangements or any significant change of circumstances occurring after the review that affects those arrangements [reg.37]

Records of Reviews [Reg.38 CPP&CR (England) Regulations 2010]

- The responsible authority must ensure that a written report of the review is produced, and that the information obtained in the course of the review, details of proceedings at the review meeting, and any decisions made in the course of or as a result of the review are included in C's case record [reg.38].

Arrangements Made by the Responsible Authority for Ceasing to Look After a Child [Regs.39–44]

Arrangements for Ceasing to Look After a Child who is Not an 'Eligible Child' [Reg.39 CPP&CR Regulations 2010]

■ In any case in which C is not a child in the care of the responsible authority and is not an 'eligible child', and her/his circumstances have changed such that the responsible authority is likely to cease to provide C with accommodation, the care plan must include details of the advice, assistance and support that the responsible authority intend to provide for C when s/he ceases to be looked after by the responsible authority [reg.39].

Eligible Child: Meaning [Reg.40 CPP&CR Regulations 2010]

■ For the purposes of para.19B (2)(b) of Sch.2 Children Act 1989 (which defines an 'eligible' child), the 'prescribed period' is 13 weeks and the 'prescribed age' is 14 [reg.40(1)].

■ If though, C is a child to whom reg.48 (short breaks) applies, C is *not* an eligible child despite falling within para.19B(2) of Schedule 2 [reg.40(2)].

NB. CAE's companion guide to the Children Act 1989 includes details of the Children (Leaving Care) Act 2000.

Eligible Child: General Duties [Reg.41 CPP&CR Regulations 2010]

- If C is an eligible child, the responsible authority:

  - Must assess her/his needs in accordance with reg. 42 and
  - Prepare C's pathway plan, in accordance with reg.43 [reg.41]

Eligible Child: Assessment of Needs [Reg.42 CPP&CR Regulations 2010]

- The responsible authority must complete the assessment of C's needs in accordance with para.19B(4) of Sch.2 Children Act 1989 not more than 3 months after the date on which s/he reaches the age of 16 or becomes an eligible child after that age [reg.42(1)].

- In carrying out its assessment of C's likely needs when it ceases to look after her/him, the responsible authority must take account of the following considerations:

  - C's state of health (including physical, emotional and mental health) and development
  - C's continuing need for education, training or employment
  - The support that will be available to C from C's parents and other connected persons
  - C's actual and anticipated financial resources and capacity to manage personal finances independently

- The extent to which C possesses the practical and other skills necessary for independent living
- C's needs for continuing needs for care, support and accommodation
- The wishes and feelings of C, any parent of C's and any person who is not C's parent but who has parental responsibility for C and the 'appropriate person'
- The views of any person or educational institution that provides C with education or training (and if C has a statement of special educational needs, the local authority that maintains the statement), the IRO, any person providing health (physical, mental or emotional health) or dental care or treatment to C, the personal adviser appointed for C, and any other person whose views the responsible authority or C consider may be relevant [reg.42(2)]

Eligible Child: Pathway Plan [Reg.43 & Sch.8 CPP&CR Regulations 2010]

- A pathway plan must be prepared as soon as possible after the assessment of C's needs and must include, in particular C's care plan and the following information referred to in Sch.8 of these regulations:

  - Name of C's personal adviser (PA)
  - Nature and level of contact and personal support to be provided to C, and by whom
  - Details of the accommodation C is to occupy when C ceases to be looked after

- Plan for C's continuing education or training when C ceases to be looked after
- How the responsible authority will assist C in obtaining employment or other purposeful activity or occupation
- Support to be provided to enable C to develop and sustain appropriate family and social relationships
- A programme to develop the practical and other skills C needs to live independently
- Financial support to be provided to enable C to meet her/his accommodation and maintenance costs
- C's health care needs, including any physical, emotional or mental health needs and how they are to be met when C ceases to be looked after.
- Responsible authority's contingency plans for action to be taken in the event that the pathway plan ceases to be effective for any reason [reg.43(1) & Sch.8]

■ The pathway plan must, in relation to the matters referred to in Sch.8 above set out the:

- Manner in which the responsible authority proposes to meet C's needs, and
- Date by which, and by whom, any action required to implement any aspect of the plan will be carried out [reg.43(2)]

Eligible Child: Functions of the Personal Adviser [Reg.44 CPP&CR Regulations 2010]

- The personal adviser in relation to C the functions to:

  - Provide advice (including practical advice) and support
  - Participate in reviews of C's case carried out under Part 6
  - Liaise with the responsible authority in the implementation of the pathway plan
  - Co-ordinate the provision of services and to take reasonable steps to ensure C makes use of such services
  - Remain informed about C's progress and wellbeing
  - Maintain a written record of contacts with C [reg.44]

Independent Reviewing Officers & Independent Visitors [Regs.45–47]

Additional Functions of Independent Reviewing Officers [Reg.45 CPP&CR (England) Regulations 2010

- The IRO must ensure that, having regard to C's age and understanding that C has been informed by the responsible authority of the steps s/he may take under the 1989 Act and in particular, when appropriate:

  - C's right to apply, with leave, for a s.8 order (Residence Contact and other orders with respect to children) and, if C is in the care of the responsible authority, to apply for the discharge of the Care Order, and
  - The availability of the procedure established under s.26(3)(a) Children Act 1989 for considering any representations (including complaints) C may wish to make about the discharge by the responsible authority of its functions, including the availability of assistance to make such representations under s.26A(b) (advocacy services) [reg.45(1)]

- If C wishes to take legal proceedings under the 1989 Act, the IRO must:

- Establish whether an appropriate adult is able and willing to assist C to obtain legal advice or bring proceedings on C's behalf, and
- If there is no such person, assist C to obtain such advice [reg.45(2)]

■ The IRO must consider whether it would be appropriate to refer C's case to an officer of the Children and Family Court Advisory and Support Service (CAFCASS) if :

- In the opinion of the IRO, the responsible authority has failed in any significant respect to make C's care plan in accordance with these regulations, review C's case in accordance with them, or to implement effectively any decision taken in consequence of a review, or is otherwise in breach of its duties to C in any material respect, and
- Having drawn the failure to the attention of persons at an appropriate level of seniority within the responsible authority, it has not been addressed to the satisfaction of the IRO within a reasonable period of time [reg.45(3)]

■ When consulted by the responsible authority about any matter concerning C, or when informed of any matter relating to C in accordance with these regulations, the IRO must:

- Ensure that the responsible authority has ascertained, and given due consideration to, C's wishes and feelings concerning the matter in question, and

- Consider whether to request a review of C's case [reg.45(4)]

Qualifications & Experience of Independent Reviewing Officers [Reg.46 CPP&CR (England) Regulations 2010]

■ The IRO must be registered as a social worker in a register maintained by the General Social Care Council (GSCC) or by the Care Council for Wales under s.56 Care Standards Act 2000 or in a corresponding register maintained under the law of Scotland or Northern Ireland [reg.46(1)].

■ The IRO must have sufficient relevant social work experience with children and families to perform the functions of an IRO set out in s.25B (1) and under these regulations in an independent manner and having regard to C's best interests [reg.46(2)].

■ The responsible authority must not appoint any of the following as the IRO:

- A person involved in preparing C's care plan or the management of C's case
- R (the local authority representative who visits C in accordance with arrangements made under s.23ZA)
- C's personal adviser
- A person with management responsibilities in relation to any of the above 3 persons

- A person with control over the resources allocated to the case [reg.46(3)]

Independent Visitors [Reg.47 CPP&CR (England) Regulations 2010

■ A person appointed by the responsible authority as an independent visitor under s.23ZB(1) is to be regarded as independent of that authority when the person appointed is not connected with the responsible authority by virtue of being:

- A member of the responsible authority or any of its committees or sub-committees, whether elected or co-opted
- An officer of the responsible authority employed in the exercise of the functions referred to in s.18(2) Children Act 2004 or
- A spouse, civil partner or other person (whether of different or same sex) living in the same household as the partner of, a person falling within either of the 2 categories above [reg.47]

Miscellaneous [Regs.48–51]

Application of These Regulations with Modifications to Short Breaks [Reg.48 CPP&CR Regulations (England) 2010]

■ In the circumstances set out in para.2, these regulations apply with the modifications set out in para.3. [reg.48(1)].

■ The circumstances are that:

- C is not in the care of the responsible authority
- The responsible authority has arranged to place C in a series of short-term placements with the same person or at the same place ('short breaks'), and
- The arrangement is such that no single placement is intended to last for more than 17 days; at the end of each such placement C returns to the care of either C's parent or a person who is not C's parent but who has parental responsibility for C and the short breaks do not exceed 75 days in total in any period of 12 months [reg.48(2)]

■ The modifications are that:

- Reg.5 (preparation and content of the care plan) and reg.9 (placement plan) do *not* apply but instead the care plan must set out the arrangements that have been made to meet C's needs, with particular regard to her/his health and emotional and behavioural development, in particular in relation to any disability C may have; promoting contact between C and C's parents and any other person who is not C's parent but who has parental responsibility for C during any period when C is placed; C's leisure interests and promoting C's educational achievement *and* must include the information set out in paras.3 and 4 of Sch.2 to these regulations, as appropriate

- Reg. 7 (health care),reg. 13 (notification of placements) and reg.49(2)(b) (case record as per reg.7) do not apply
- Reg. 28(2) (frequency of visits by a representative of the responsible authority) does not apply, but instead the responsible authority must ensure its representative visits C on a day when s/he is in fact placed, at regular intervals to be agreed with the IRO and C's parents (or any person who is not C's parent but who has parental responsibility for C), and recorded in the care plan before the start of the first placement, and in any event the first visit must take place within 3 months of the start of the placement or as soon as practicable thereafter and subsequent visits at intervals of not more than 6 months for as long as the short breaks continue
- Reg.33 (timing of reviews) does not apply, but instead the responsible authority must first review C's case within 3 months of the beginning of the first placement, and the second and

subsequent reviews must be carried out at intervals of no more than 6 months thereafter [reg.48(3)]

Records: Establishment [Reg.49 CPP&CR Regulations (England) 2010]

■ The responsible authority must establish and maintain a written case record for C, if one is not already in existence [reg.49(1)] (see page 20).

■ The record must include:

- C's care plan, including any changes made to the care plan and any subsequent plans
- Reports obtained under reg.7 (health care)
- Any other document created or considered as part of any assessment of C's needs or of any review of C's case
- Any court order relating to C
- Details of any arrangements have been made by the responsible authority with any other local authority or with an independent fostering agency (IFA) under reg.26 and Sch.5 or with a provider of social work services under which any of the responsible authority's functions in relation to C are discharged by that local authority or IFA or provider of social work services, details of those arrangements [reg.49(2)]

Records: Retention & Confidentiality Reg.50 CPP&CR Regulations (England) 2010]

- The responsible authority must retain the case record relating to C either:

  - Until the 75th anniversary of C's birth, or
  - If C dies before attaining the age of 18, for 15 years beginning with the date of C's death [reg.50(1)]

- The responsible authority must secure the safe keeping of C's case record and take any necessary steps to ensure that information contained in it is treated as confidential subject only to any:

  - Provision of or made under or by virtue of, a statute under which access to such records or information may be obtained or given
  - Court order under which access to such records or information may be obtained or given [reg.50(2)]

Records: Children in an 'Area Authority'

- Statutory guidance (page 48 Volume 2) indicates that an Area Authority should maintain a list of all the notifications of looked after children placed in its area so that it can fulfil its statutory duties under the Children Act 1989.

CHILDREN'S HOMES
REGULATIONS

General [Regs. 1–5 Children's Homes Regulations 2001]

■ The registered person in relation to a children's home means any person who is the registered provider or registered manager of that home.

■ The registered manager in relation to a children's home means a person who is registered under Part II of the CSA 2000 as the manager of that home

■ The registered provider in relation to a children's home means a person who is registered under Part II of the CSA 2000 as the person carrying on that home.

■ 'Designated teacher' has the meaning given to it in reg.2 Designated Teacher (Looked After Pupils etc) (England) Regulations 2009 i.e. a member of staff at a maintained school designated by the governors' body for purposes of s.20(1) C&YP 2008.

Excepted Establishments [Reg. 3 Children's Homes Regulations 2001 (as amended)]

■ The following are excepted from being a children's home:

- Any institution within the further education sector as defined by s.91(3) Further and Higher Education Act 1992
- Any establishment providing accommodation for children for fewer than 28 days in any 12 months

in relation to any 1 child for purposes of a holiday or recreational, sporting, cultural or educational activity

- Any premises at which a person provides childcare within the meaning of s.18 Childcare Act 2006 for fewer than 28 days in any 12 month period in relation to any 1 child
- Any establishment providing accommodation for children aged 16 or over to enable them to undergo training or apprenticeship, for a holiday or for recreational, cultural or educational purposes
- Any approved bail or probation hostel
- Any institution provided for young offenders under or by virtue of s.43(1) Prison Act 1952

NB. The exceptions in roundels 2–4 inc. above do not apply if the children accommodated are wholly or mainly 'of a description falling within s.3(2) CSA 2000' i.e. they have physical or mental illnesses, are disabled or have been dependent on drugs or alcohol.

For purposes of calculating the 28 days specified in the third roundel above, no account is taken of any period of 24 hours during which at least 9 are spent by a child in the care of her/his parent or relative and childcare is not being provided for the child during that time.

Statement of Purpose and Children's Guide [Regs. 4, 5 & Sch. 1 Children's Homes Regulations 2001 (as amended)]

■ The registered person must compile a 'statement of purpose' which includes:

- The overall aims of the home and objectives to be attained with respect to residents
- A statement of facilities and services to be provided
- Name and address of registered provider and registered manager if applicable
- Relevant qualifications and experience of persons working at the home, and if workers all of same sex, a description of the means whereby the home will promote appropriate role models of both sexes
- Arrangements for supervision, training and development of employees
- Organisational structure of the home
- Particulars about age range, sex, numbers of residents, whether it is intended to accommodate disabled children, those with special needs or nay other special characteristics and the range of other needs the home is intended to meet
- Admission criteria, including home's policy and procedures (where relevant) for emergency admissions
- A description of the home's underlying ethos and philosophy and where this is based upon any

theoretical or therapeutic model, a description of that model
- Arrangements made to protect and promote the health of children
- Arrangements for promotion of the education of residents including the facilities for private study
- Arrangements to promote children's participation in recreational, sporting and cultural activities
- Arrangements made for consultation with residents about the operation of the home
- Arrangements made for promoting the appropriate behaviour of children and for the control, restraint and discipline of children
- Arrangements made for child protection and to counter bullying
- Procedure for dealing with any incident where a child goes missing from the home
- A description of any electronic or mechanical means of surveillance which may be used
- Fire precautions and associated emergency procedures
- Arrangements for contact between child and parents, relatives and friends
- Arrangements for dealing with complaints
- Details of any specific therapeutic techniques used and arrangements for their supervision
- A description of the homes policy in relation to anti-discriminatory practice as respects children and children's rights [reg.4(1); Sch.1]

■ The registered person must provide a copy of the statement of purpose to the Chief Inspector and make a copy of it available upon request for its inspection, by:

- Any person who works at the home
- Any actual or potential resident
- The parent of any resident
- The placing authority
- (In the case of a 'qualifying school') the Secretary of State and Her Majesty's Inspector of Schools in England [reg.4(2)]

▪ The registered person must also produce a 'children's guide' to the home which includes:

- A summary of the home's statement of purpose
- A summary of the reg. 24 complaints procedure
- Address and telephone number of the Chief Inspector [reg.4(3)]

▪ The children's guide must be produced in a form appropriate to the age, understanding and communication needs of residents [reg.4(4).

▪ The registered person must supply a copy of the children's guide to the Chief inspector and, on admission, to each child accommodated in the home [reg.4(5)]

▪ Subject to reg 4 (7) the registered person must ensure the home is at all times conducted in a manner which is consistent with it's statement of purpose [reg.4(6)]

▪ Nothing in reg.4 (6) or reg.31 must require or authorise the registered person to contravene or not

comply with any other provision of these regulations
or conditions for the time being in force in relation to
the registration of the registered person under part 2
of the CSA 2000.[reg.4 (7)]

Review of Statement of Purpose and Children's Guide [Reg 5 Children's Homes Regulations (as Amended)]

- The registered person must keep under review and
  when appropriate, revise the statement of purpose
  and children's guide, notify the Chief Inspector within
  28 days of any such revision and ensure that
  residents receive the updated children's guide.

Registered Persons [Regs. 6–10 Children's Homes Regulations 2001 (as amended)]

Fitness of Registered Provider [Reg. 6 Children's Homes Regulations 2001 (as amended)]

- ■ A person must not carry on a children's home unless s/he is fit to do so [reg.6(1)].

- ■ A person is not fit to carry on a home trading either as an individual, a partner or an organisation unless all specified requirements are satisfied [reg.6(2)].

  NB. In the case of an organisation it must give notice to the Chief Inspector of the name address and position in the organisation of an individual (the responsible individual) who is a director, manager, secretary or other officer of the organisation and is responsible for supervising of the home

- ■ The requirements are that:

  - • Each individual is of integrity and good character
  - • S/he is physically and mentally fit to carry on a home
  - • Full and satisfactory information is available about the person as detailed in paras. 1 and 3–7 Sch. 2 Children's Homes Regulations 2001 (as amended) (see below) [reg.6(3)]

- ■ A person is not allowed to carry on a children's home if s/he is an un-discharged bankrupt or has made an arrangement with creditors in respect of which s/he has not been discharged [reg.6(5)].

Appointment of Manager [Reg. 7 Children's Homes Regulations 2001 (as amended)]

■ The registered provider must appoint an individual to manage the home if:

- There is no registered manager for the home and
- The registered provider is an organisation or partnership, is not a fit person to manage a children's home or is not or does not intend to be in full-time day to day charge of the home [reg.7(1)]

■ Where the registered provider appoints a person to manage the children's home, s/he must immediately give notice to the Chief Inspector of:

- The name of the person so appointed and
- The date on which the appointment is to take effect [reg.7(2)]

Fitness of Manager [Reg. 8 Children's Homes Regulations 2001 (as amended)]

■ A person must not manage a children's home unless s/he is fit to do so [reg.8(1)].

■ A person is not fit to manage a children's home unless:

- S/he is of integrity and good character

- Having regard to the size of the children's home, its statement of purpose, the number and needs (including any needs arising from any disability) of the children accommodated there, s/he has the qualifications, skills and experience necessary for managing the children's home; and is physically and mentally fit to manage the children's home; and
- Full and satisfactory information is available in relation to him in respect of each of the matters specified in Sch.2 reg.8(2).

Information Required in Respect of Persons Seeking to Carry On, Manage or Work at a Children's Home [Sch.2 in Support of Regs. 6, 8 & 26 Children's Homes Regulations 2001 (as amended)]

■ Proof of identity including a recent photograph.

■ Where the certificate is required for a purpose related to registration under Part 2 of the Act or the position falls within regulation 5A Police Act 1997 (Criminal Records) Regulations 2002, an enhanced criminal record certificate issued under s.113B Police Act 1997 which includes suitability information relating to children (within the meaning of s.113BA(2) of that Act) and, where applicable, suitability information relating to vulnerable adults (within the meaning of s.113BB(2) of that Act); or in any other case, a criminal record certificate issued under s.113A Police Act 1997].

■ 2 written references, including a reference from the person's most recent employer, if any.

■ If a person has previously worked in a position whose duties involved work with children or vulnerable adults, so far as reasonably practicable verification of the reason why the employment or position ended.

■ Documentary evidence of any relevant qualifications.

■ A full employment history, together with a satisfactory written explanation of any gaps in employment [Sch.2]

Registered Person – General Requirements [Reg. 9 Children's Homes Regulations 2001 (as amended)]

■ The registered provider and the registered manager must, having regard to the home's size, statement of purpose, and number and needs of residents (including those arising from disability) carry on/ manage the home with sufficient care, competence and skill.

■ From time to time, so as to ensure sufficient experience and skills necessary for carrying on the home, appropriate training must be completed by:

- The registered provider (if s/he is an individual)
- The responsible Individual (and the responsibility for ensuring this rests with the organisation which engages her/him)

- (When relevant) 1 member of any partnership [reg.9(1)]

■ The registered manager must also undertake from time to time such training as is appropriate to ensure s/he has the experience and skills necessary for managing the children's home [reg.9(2)].

Notification of Offences [Reg. 10 Children's Homes Regulations 2001 (as amended)]

■ Where the registered person or the responsible individual is convicted of any criminal offence in England or Wales or elsewhere, s/he must immediately give notice to the Chief Inspector of the:

- Date and place of the conviction
- Offence of which s/he was convicted
- Penalty imposed

Welfare of Children [Regs. 11–24]

Promotion of Welfare [Reg. 11 Children's Homes Regulations 2001 (as amended)]

■ The registered person must ensure that the home is conducted so as to:

- Promote and make proper provision for the welfare of residents
- Make proper provision for care, education, supervision and where appropriate treatment of residents [reg.11(1)]

■ The registered person must make suitable arrangements to ensure the home is conducted, with respect to children accommodated there:

- In a manner which respects their privacy and dignity
- With due regard to their sex, religious persuasion, racial origin and cultural and linguistic background and any disability [reg.11(2)]

Placement Plan for a Child who is Not Looked After [Reg.12 Children's Homes Regulations 2001 (as amended)]

■ If a child who is not looked after by a local authority is placed in a children's home by a voluntary organisation, the registered person must co-operate with the voluntary organisation in agreeing and signing the placement plan prepared for the child in accordance with regs.4&5 of the Arrangement for Placement of Children by Voluntary Organisations and Others (England) 2011 [reg.12 (1)].

■ If a child who is not looked after by a local authority is placed in a private children's home other than by a voluntary organisation, the registered person must prepare a placement plan for her/him in accordance with regs.4 & 5 of the 2011 regs. [reg.12 (1A)]

■ In all other cases, the registered person must before providing accommodation in a children's home for a child not looked after by a local authority, or if not reasonably practicably, as soon as possible thereafter, prepare in consultation with the child's placing authority, a placement plan setting out in particular:

  • How on a day to day basis the child will be cared for and her/his welfare safeguarding and promoted by the home
  • Arrangements made for the child's health care and education and
  • Arrangements made for contact with the child's parents, relatives and friends [reg.12 (1B)].

N.B. In reg.12 private children's home means a home in respect of which is registered under part 2 CSA 2000 which is not a community or voluntary home [reg.12 (5)].

Placement Plan for Looked After Child [Reg.12A]

■ In the case of a child who is looked after by a local authority the registered person must co-operate with the child's placing authority in agreeing and signing the plan for the child's placement in accordance with the provision of reg. 9 care planning regulation [reg.12A(1)].

■ The registered person must comply with requests by the child's placing authority to;

- Provide it with information to the child and
- Provide a suitable representative for any meetings it may hold concerning the child [reg.12A(2)].

Food Provided [Reg. 13 Children's Homes Regulations 2001 (as amended)]

■ The registered person must ensure that the children accommodated are provided with access to fresh drinking water at all times and food which is:

- Served in adequate quantities at appropriate intervals
- Properly prepared, wholesome and nutritious
- Suitable for their needs and meets reasonable preferences
- Is sufficiently varied [reg.13(1)]

■ The registered person must ensure any special dietary need of an accommodated child due to her/his health, religious persuasion, racial origin or cultural background is met [reg.13(2)].

Provision of Clothing, Pocket Money & Personal Necessities [Reg. 14 Children's Homes Regulations 2001 (as amended)]

■ The registered person must ensure that the needs and reasonable preferences of each resident for clothing, including footwear and personal necessities are met [reg.14(1)].

■ The registered person must provide residents with such sums of money for occasional personal expenses as are appropriate to their age and understanding [reg.14(2)].

Contact & Access to Communication [Reg. 15 Children's Homes Regulations 2001 (as amended)]

■ The registered person must (unless exceptions specified in the final paragraph below apply) promote contact of each child with her/his parents, relatives and friends in accordance with arrangements in the placement plan [reg.15(1)].

■ Except in the case of a certified 'refuge', (when they may be at a different address) the registered person must ensure suitable facilities are provided within the home for any resident to meet privately at any reasonable time her/his parents, relatives and friends and the following individuals:

• Any solicitor/other adviser/advocate for the child
• Any CAFCASS officer appointed for her/him

- Any social worker assigned to the child by the placing authority
- Any person appointed in connection with an investigation of a complaint
- Any independent visitor
- Any person authorised by the Chief Inspector
- Any person authorised by the local authority in whose area the home is situated
- Any person authorised by Secretary of State to inspect the home and the children there [reg.15(2);(3)]

■ The registered person must ensure that residents are provided at all reasonable times with access to the following facilities which they may use in private without reference to persons working in the home:

- A telephone on which to make and receive calls
- A capacity to send and receive post and (where available) e-mails [reg.15(4)]

■ The registered person must ensure any resident is provided with access to such aids and equipment which s/he may require as a result of her/his disability in order to facilitate communication with others [reg.15(5)].

■ The registered person *may* though impose such restriction, prohibition or condition upon a child's contact or access to communications which s/he is satisfied is necessary for the purpose of safeguarding or promoting the welfare of the child in question only if:

- The child's placing authority consents to the imposition of the measure or
- The measure is imposed in an emergency and full details are given to the placing authority with 24 hours of its imposition [reg.15(6);(7)]

NB. Reg. 15 is subject to the provisions of any relevant court order relating to contact between child and any person [reg.15(8)].

Arrangements for Protection of Children [Reg. 16 Children's Homes Regulations 2001 (as amended)]

- The registered person must prepare and implement a written policy which:

    - Is intended to safeguard children accommodated in the children's home from abuse or neglect and
    - Sets out the procedure to be followed in the event of any allegation or abuse or neglect [reg.16(1)]

- The child protection procedures must in particular provide for:

    - Liaison and co-operation with any local authority which is or may be making child protection enquiries in relation to any resident
    - Prompt referral to the local authority in whose area the home is situated, of any allegation of abuse or neglect affecting any accommodated child

- Notification (in accordance with reg. 30) of instigation and outcome of any child protection enquiries involving any child accommodated to the Chief Inspector and the child's placing authority
- Written records to be kept of any allegations of abuse or neglect, and of any action taken in response
- Consideration to be given to measures which may be necessary to protect children in the home following an allegation of abuse or neglect
- A requirement for persons working at the home to report any concerns about the welfare or safety of an accommodated child to either the registered person, a police officer, an officer of the Chief Inspector, an officer of the local authority where the home is situated or an officer of the NSPCC
- Arrangements to be made for persons working in the home and residents to have access at all times and in an appropriate form, to information that would enable them (in the event that they were concerned about a resident child's welfare or safety) to contact the local authority where the home is, or the Chief Inspector [reg.16(2)]

NB. In this regulation 'child protection enquiries' means any enquiries carried out by a local authority in the exercise of any of its functions conferred by or under the 1989 Act relating to the protection of children [reg.16(3)]

■ The registered person must also prepare and implement as required a:

- Policy for the prevention of bullying in the home which must in particular include the procedure for dealing with an allegation of bullying
- Procedure to be followed when any resident is missing without permission having regard to any relevant local authority or police protocols on missing children [reg.16(4)]

Behaviour Management, Discipline and Restraint [Reg. 17 Children's Homes Regulations 2001 (as amended)]

■ No measure of control or discipline which is excessive, unreasonable or contrary to reg.17(2) must be used at any time on children accommodated in a children's home [reg.17(1)].

■ Subject to reg.17(3), the following shall not be used as disciplinary measures on children accommodated in a children's home:

- Any form of corporal punishment
- Any punishment involving the consumption or deprivation of food or drink
- Any restriction, other than one imposed by a court or in accordance with reg.15, on a child's contact with parents, relatives or friends; visits to the child by the child's parents, relatives or friends; a child's communications with any of the persons listed in reg. 15(2); or a child's access to

any telephone helpline providing counselling for children

- Any requirement that a child wear distinctive or inappropriate clothes
- Use or withholding of medication or medical or dental treatment
- Intentional deprivation of sleep
- Imposition of any financial penalty, other than a requirement for the payment of a reasonable sum (which may be by instalments) by way of reparation
- Any intimate physical examination of the child
- Withholding of any aids or equipment needed by a disabled child
- Any measure which involves any child in the imposition of any measure against any other child; or the punishment of a group of children for the behaviour of an individual child [reg.17(2)]

■ Nothing in this regulation prohibits:

- Taking of any action by, or in accordance with the instructions of, a general medical practitioner or a registered dental practitioner which is necessary to protect the health of a child
- Taking of any action immediately necessary to prevent injury to any person or serious damage to property; or
- Imposition of a requirement that a child wear distinctive clothing for sporting purposes, or for purposes connected with her/his education or

with any organisation whose members customarily wear uniform in connection with its activities [reg.17(3)]

Restraint [Reg. 17A Children's Homes Regulations 2001 (as amended)]

■ Subject to reg.17A(2) and then *only* when no alternative method of preventing the event specified below is available, a measure of restraint *may* be used on a child accommodated in a children's home for the purpose of:

- Preventing injury to any person (including the child who is being restrained)
- Preventing serious damage to the property of any person (including the child who is being restrained) and
- In the case of a child accommodated in a children's home which is a secure children's home, preventing the child from absconding from the home [reg.17A(1)]

■ If a measure of restraint is used on a child accommodated in a children's home:

- The measure of restraint must be proportionate, and
- No more force than is necessary should be used [reg.17A(2)]

NB. In reg.17A a 'secure children's home' means a children's home used for the purpose of restricting liberty and approved for that purpose in respect of which a person is registered under Part 2 of the Care Standards Act 2000 [reg.17A(3)].

Policies & Records [Reg. 17B Children's Homes Regulations 2001 (as amended)]

- The registered person shall prepare and implement a written policy (in this regulation referred to as the 'behaviour management policy') which sets out the:

  - Measures of control, restraint and discipline which may be used in the children's home; and
  - Means whereby appropriate behaviour is to be promoted in the home [reg.17B(1)]

- The registered person must:

  - Keep under review and where appropriate revise the behaviour management policy; and
  - Notify the Chief Inspector of any such revision within 28 days [reg.17B(2)]

- The registered person must ensure that within 24 hours of the use of any measure of control, restraint or discipline in a children's home, a written record is made in a volume kept for the purpose which must include:

  - The name of the child concerned
  - Details of the child's behaviour leading to the use of the measure
  - A description of the measure used
  - Date, time and location of, the use of the measure

- Name of the person using the measure, and of any other person present
- The effectiveness and any consequences of the use of the measure
- A description of any injury to the child concerned or any other person and any medical treatment administered
- Confirmation that the person authorised by the registered provider to make the record has spoken to the child concerned and the person using the measure about the use of the measure, and
- The signature of a person authorised by the registered provider to make the record [reg.17B(3)]

■ When a measure of restraint is used on a child the record required under reg.17B(3) must include:

- The duration of the restraint and
- Details of any methods used to avoid the need to use that measure [reg.17B(4)]

Education, Employment & Leisure Activity [Reg. 18 Children's Homes Regulations 2001 (as amended)]

■ The registered person must promote the educational achievement of children accommodated in a children's home, in particular by ensuring that:

- Children make use of educational facilities appropriate to age, aptitude, needs, interests and potential
- The routine of the home is organised so as to further children's participation in education, including private study and to ensure regular attendance at school and participation in school activities for children of compulsory school age and regular attendance at college where applicable
- Effective links are maintained with any schools/colleges attended by children accommodated [reg.18(1)]

■ The registered person must ensure that residents are:

- Encouraged to develop and pursue appropriate leisure interests and
- Provided with appropriate leisure facilities and activities [reg.18(2)]

■ When any child in a children's home has attained the age where s/he is no longer required to receive compulsory full-time education, the registered person must assist with making and implementing arrangements for her/his education, training and employment [reg.18(3)].

Religious Observance [s.19 Children's Homes Regulations 2001]

■ The registered person must ensure that each accommodated child is enabled, so far as practicable with respect her/his religious persuasion, to:

- Attend services
- Receive instruction
- Observe any requirements as to dress, diet or otherwise [reg.19]

Health Needs of Children [Reg. 20 Children's Homes Regulations 2001 (as amended)]

■ The registered person must promote and protect the physical, emotional and mental health of residents and in particular ensure that:

- Each child is a registered patient with a general medical practitioner who provides primary medical services under Part 4 NHS Act 2006 and has access to such medical, dental, nursing, psychological and psychiatric advice, treatment and other services as s/he may require
- Each child is provided with such individual support, aids and equipment as s/he may require as result of any particular health needs or disability
- Each child is provided with guidance, support and advice on health and personal care issues appropriate to her/his needs and wishes

- At all times, at least 1 person on duty at the home has a suitable first aid qualification
- Any person appointed to the position of nurse at the children's home is a registered nurse [reg.20(1);(2)]

Medicines [Reg. 21 Children's Homes Regulations 2001 (as amended)]

■ The registered person must make suitable arrangements for the recording, handling, safekeeping, safe administration and disposal of any medicines received into the home [reg.21(1)].

■ In particular the registered person must (unless it is stored by the child for whom it is intended in such a way that others are prevented from using it, and may be self-administered) ensure that:

- Any medicine kept in the home is stored in a secure place so as to prevent any resident having unsupervised access to it
- Any prescribed medicine is administered as prescribed only to the child for whom intended
- A written record is kept of the administration of any medicine to any child [reg.21(2);(3)]

Use of Surveillance [Reg. 22 Children's Homes Regulations 2001 (as amended)]

■ Subject to any requirements for electronic monitoring imposed by a court under any law, the registered person must ensure that electronic or mechanical monitoring devices for surveillance of children are not used in the home, except for the purpose of safeguarding and promoting the welfare of the child concerned or other residents and where the following conditions are met:

- The child's placing authority consent
- It is provided for in the child's placement plan
- So far as practicable in the light of her/his age and understanding, the child in question is informed in advance of the intention to use the measure and
- The measure is not more restrictive than necessary, having regard to the child's needs for privacy [reg.22(1)]

■ The conditions in reg.22(1) do not apply to a secure children's home [reg.22(2)].

Hazards & Safety [Reg. 23 Children's Homes Regulations 2001 (as amended)]

■ The registered person must ensure that:

- All parts of the home to which the children have access are as far as reasonably practicable free from hazards to their health or safety and
- Any activities in which children participate are so far as reasonably practicable free from avoidable risks [reg.23]

Complaints & Representations [Reg. 24 Children's Homes Regulations 2001 (as amended)]

- For issues not covered by the Children Act Representation Procedure (England) Regulations 2006 (which enable them to initiate formal suggestions and complaints about services offered or not offered by a local authority, reg. 24 offers residents in children's homes, an additional right to complain.

- The registered person must establish a written procedure for considering complains made by or on behalf of children accommodated in the home [reg.24(1)].

- The procedure must in particular provide:

  - An opportunity for informal resolution of the complaint at an early stage
  - That no person who is subject of a complaint takes any part in its consideration other than if the registered person considers it appropriate, at the informal resolution stage only
  - For complaints about the registered person
  - For complaints to be made by a person acting on behalf of a child
  - For arrangements for the procedure to be made known to residents, their parents, placing authorities and persons working in the home reg.24[2)]

- A copy of the procedure must be supplied on request to any of the above individuals and must include:

- Name, address and telephone number of the Chief Inspector and
- Details of the procedure (if any) which has been notified to the registered person by the Chief Inspector for the making of complaints to it relating to the home [reg.24(3);(4)]

■ The registered person must ensure that a written record is made of any complaint, the action taken in response and the outcome of the investigation [reg.24(5)]

■ The registered person must ensure that:

- Children accommodated in the home are enabled to make a complaint or representation and
- No child is subject to any reprisal for so doing [reg.24(6)]

■ The registered person must supply to the Chief Inspector a statement containing a summary of any complaints made in preceding 12 months and the action that was taken [reg.24(7)].

NB. The procedure in reg.24(1) may be kept in electronic form provided the information so recorded is capable of being reproduced in a legible form [reg.24(9)].

Staffing [Regs. 25–27]

Numbers & Fitness [Regs. 25, 26 Children's Homes Regulations 2001]

■ The registered person must ensure that there is at all times a sufficient number of suitably qualified, competent and experienced persons working at the home, having regard to the:

- Size of the home, its statement of purpose and the number and needs (including any arising from any disability) of residents
- Need to safeguard and promote the health and welfare of the residents [reg.25(1)]

■ The registered person must ensure that the employment of any persons on a temporary basis at the home will not prevent the children from receiving such continuity of care as is reasonable to meet their needs [reg.25(2)]

■ The registered person must not, unless the person in question is fit to work at a children's home:

- Employ a person to work at the home or
- Allow a person who is employed by someone other than the registered person to work at the home in a position in which s/he may in the course of her/his duties have regular contact with residents [reg.26(1)]

■ A person is not fit to work at a children's home unless:

- S/he is of integrity and good character
- Has the qualifications, skills and experience necessary for the work s/he is to perform
- Is physically and mentally fit for the purposes of the work to be performed and
- Full and satisfactory information is available about the person as per paras. 1 and 3–7 of Sch. 2 (see page 94) [reg.26(3)]

■ The registered person must ensure that:

- Any offer of employment is subject to requirements of the final bullet point above being satisfied
- Unless the circumstances described below apply, no person starts work at a children's home until such time as those requirements have been satisfied [reg.26(5)]

■ Where the following criteria apply, the registered person *may* permit a person to start work at a children's home *if*:

- S/he has taken all reasonable steps to obtain full information in respect of each of the matters listed in Sch. 2 but enquiries in relation to any matters listed in paras. 3–6 are incomplete i.e. 2 references, verification of reasons for termination of previous comparable work, evidence of relevant qualifications, full employment history
- Full and satisfactory information in respect of that person has been obtained in relation to

- para. 1 Sch. 2 (proof of identity including a recent photo) and
- Full and satisfactory information in respect of that person has been obtained in relation to para. 2 of Sch. 2 and
- Full and satisfactory information in respect of that person has been obtained in relation to para. 7 of Sch. 2 (all convictions and cautions)
- The registered person considers that the circumstances are exceptional and pending receipt of satisfactory information, s/he ensures that the person is appropriately supervised while carrying out her/his duties [reg.26(6)]

■ The registered person must also take reasonable steps to ensure that any person, other than one already specified above who works at a children's home is appropriately supervised while carrying out her/his duties [reg.26(7)]. (The published regulations erroneously label this as reg 26(6).)

Employment of Staff [Reg. 27 Children's Homes Regulations 2001 (as amended)]

■ The registered person must:

- Ensure all permanent appointments are subject to the satisfactory completion of a period of probation and
- Provide all employees with a job description outlining their responsibilities [reg.27(1)]

- The registered person must operate a disciplinary procedure which, in particular:

  - Provides for the suspension of an employee when necessary in the interests of the safety or welfare of children accommodated in the home
  - Provides that the failure on the part of an employee to report an incident of abuse, or suspected abuse, of a resident to an appropriate person (the registered person, an officer of the Chief Inspector, local authority in which home is situated or a police officer) is a ground on which disciplinary proceedings may be instituted [reg.27(2);(3)]

- The registered person must ensure that all persons employed by her/him:

  - Receive appropriate training, supervision and appraisal and
  - Are enabled from time to time to obtain further qualifications appropriate to the work they perform [reg.27(4)]

Records [Regs. 28–30]

Children's Case Records [Reg. 28 & Sch.3 Children's Homes Regulations 2001 (as amended)]

- The registered person must maintain in respect of each accommodated child a permanent record which:

  - Includes the information, documents and records specified in Sch. 3 (see below) relating to that child
  - Is kept up to date and
  - Is signed and dated by the author of each entry [reg.28(1)]

- Sch. 3 specifies the following:

  - Current and any previous name (other than a name used prior to adoption)
  - Sex and date of birth
  - Child's religious persuasion if any
  - Racial origin, cultural and linguistic background
  - Address immediately prior to entering the home
  - Name, address and telephone number of child's placing authority
  - Statutory provision (if any) under which s/he is provided with accommodation
  - Name, address, phone number and religion (if any) of child's parents
  - Name, address and phone number of her/his social worker from the placing authority

- Date and circumstance of all incidents when a child accommodated in the home goes missing including any information relating to the child's whereabouts during the period of absence
- A copy of any statement of special educational needs being maintained under s.324 Education Act 1996 and details
- Date and circumstance of any measures of control, restraint or discipline used on the child
- Any special dietary or health needs
- Name and address of any school (if the school has a designated teacher her/his phone number) or college attended or of an employer
- Name, address and telephone number of any school or college attended by the child, and of any employer of the child
- Every school report received while resident
- Arrangements for, including any restrictions on, contact between child and parents, and any other person
- A copy of any plan for the care of the child prepared by the placing authority and of the placement plan
- Date and result of any review of the placing authority's plan for the care of the child, or of her/his placement plan
- Name and address of the general medical practitioner with whom the child is a registered patient, address of the premises at which the primary medical services are usually provided

and name and address of the child's dental practitioner

- Details of any accident or serious illness involving the child while accommodated in the home
- Details of any immunisation, allergy or medical examination details, any medical or dental needs or treatment of the child
- Details of any health examination or developmental test conducted with respect to the child at, or in connection with her/his school
- Details of any medicine kept for the child in the home, including any which the child is permitted to self-administer and details of administration of any medicine to her/him
- Dates on which money or valuables deposited by or on behalf of a resident for safekeeping and dates on which any money is withdrawn and any valuable returned
- Address and type of establishment or accommodation to which the child goes when s/he ceases to be accommodated in the home

■ The above record may not be disclosed to any person except in accordance with:

- Any legal provision which may make access to it lawful or
- Any court order authorising access to such records [reg.28(2)]

■ The above record must be:

- Kept securely in the home so long as the child to whom it relates is accommodated there and
- Thereafter retained in a place of security for at least 75 years from date of birth, or if s/he dies before 18 years of age, for 15 years from date of death [reg.28(3)]

■ The above records may be kept in electronic form provided it the information so recorded is capable of being reproduced in a legible form [reg.28(4)].

Other Records [Reg. 29 & Sch. 4 Children's Homes Regulations 2001 (as amended)]

■ The registered person must maintain and keep up to date, in the home the following records:

- Date of child's admission to the home
- Date on which child ceased to be accommodated
- Address prior to being accommodated in the home and address on leaving the home
- Placing authority and statutory provisions (if any) under which the child is accommodated
- A record showing for each person working at the home full name, sex, date of birth, home address, qualifications relevant to and experience of work involving children
- Whether s/he works at the home full or part-time (paid or not) and if part-time the average number of hours worked per week
- Whether s/he resides at the home
- A record of any persons who reside or work at any time at the home, who are not mentioned in

the records kept in accordance with the first two bullet points above
- A record of all accidents occurring in the home, or to children whilst accommodated by the home
- A record of the receipt, disposal and administration of any medicine to any child
- A record of every fire drill or alarm test conducted, with details of any deficiency in either the procedure or equipment concerned, taught with details of the steps taken to remedy that deficiency
- A record of all money deposited by a child for safekeeping, together with the date on which that money was withdrawn, or the date of its return
- A record of all valuables deposited by a child their date of return
- Records of all accounts kept in the children's home
- A copy of the staff duty roster of persons working at the home and a record of the actual rosters worked
- A record of all visitors to the home and to children accommodated, including the names of visitors and reasons for the visit [reg.29(1) & Sch.4]

- The above records must be retained for at least 15 years from the date of the last entry, except for records of menus which need be kept for only 1 year [reg.29(2)]

Notifiable Events [Reg. 30 & Sch. 5 Children's Homes Regulations 2001 (as amended)]

■ If any of the events below takes place, the registered person must without delay notify the persons indicated.

■ If a resident dies the following people must be notified and provided with all known details:

- The Chief Inspector
- Placing authority
- Secretary of State
- Local authority
- Primary Care Trust

■ A referral to the Secretary of State pursuant to s.2(1)(a) of Protection of Children Act 1999 of an individual working in the home must be referred to the:

- The Chief Inspector
- Placing authority

■ A serious illness or serious accident sustained by a resident must be notified to the:

- The Chief Inspector
- Placing authority

■ An outbreak of any infectious disease which in the opinion of doctor attending residents is sufficiently serious must be notified to the:

- The Chief Inspector
- Placing authority

■ An allegation that a child accommodated at the home has committed a serious offence must be notified to the:

- Placing authority
- Police

■ Involvement or suspected involvement of a resident in prostitution must be notified to the:

- The Chief Inspector
- Placing authority
- Local authority
- Police

■ A serious incident necessitating calling the police to the home must be notified to the:

- The Chief Inspector
- Placing authority

■ A child accommodated at the home who goes missing must be notified to the:

- Placing authority

■ Any serious complaint about the home or persons working there must be notified to the:

- The Chief Inspector
- Placing authority

■ Instigation and outcome of any child protection enquiries involving a resident must be notified to the:

- The Chief Inspector
- Placing authority [reg.30 (1) & Sch.5]

■ The registered person must also without delay, notify the parent of any child accommodated in the home of any significant incident affecting the child's welfare unless to do so is not reasonably practicable or would place the child's welfare at risk [reg.30(2)].

NB. Any notification made in accordance with reg.30 which is given orally must be confirmed in writing [reg.30(3)].

Premises [Regs. 31 & 32]

Fitness of Premises [Reg. 31 Children's Homes Regulations 2001 (as amended)]

■ The registered person must not use premises as a children's home unless they are in a location, and of a physical design and layout, which are suitable for the purpose of achieving the aims and objectives set out in the home's statement of purpose [reg.31(1)].

■ The registered person must ensure that all parts of the home are secure from unauthorised access [reg.31(2)].

■ The registered person must provide suitable washing, kitchen and laundry facilities for use by staff and, when appropriate, by children accommodated there [reg.31(3)].

■ The registered person must ensure the children's home is suitably furnished with adequate living, storage and communal space to:

- Meet the needs of the children accommodated
- Achieve the aims and objectives set out in the statement of purpose [reg.31(4)]

■ The registered person must ensure that having regard to her/his need for privacy each resident is provided with sleeping accommodation which is suitable for her/his needs and there are within the children's home for use by residents in conditions of appropriate privacy, a sufficient number of lavatories, wash basins, baths and showers for the number and sex of children accommodated [reg.31(5)].

■ The registered person must ensure that no child shares a bedroom with an adult, nor (except in the case of siblings) a child who is of the opposite sex or of a significantly different age to her/him [reg.31(6)].

■ The registered person must provide for persons working at the home:

- Suitable facilities and accommodation, other than sleeping accommodation including those for the purposes of changing and storage
- Sleeping accommodation where this is necessary for work purposes [reg.31(7)]

Fire Precautions [Reg. 32 Children's Homes Regulations 2001 (as amended)]

■ Subject to reg.32, the registered person must, after consultation with the fire and rescue authority:

- Take adequate precautions against the risk of fire including the provision of fire equipment
- Provide adequate means of escape
- Make arrangements for persons working at the home to receive suitable training in fire prevention
- Ensure by means of fire drills and practices at suitable intervals, that those working at the home, and so far as practicable, the residents, are

aware of the procedure to be followed in case of fire [reg.32(1)]

NB. When the Regulatory Reform (Fire Safety) Order 2005 applies to the children's home, reg.32(1) does not apply and the registered person must ensure that the requirements of that Order and any regulations made under it (except for article 23 – duties of employees – are complied with in respect of the home [re.32(1A)].

Management of Home [Regs.33–36]

Visits by Registered Provider [Reg. 33 Children's Homes Regulations 2001 (as amended)]

■ If the registered provider is an individual, but is not in day to day charge of the home, s/he must visit in accordance with this regulation [reg.33(1)].

■ If the registered provider is an organisation or a partnership, the home must be visited in accordance with this regulation by:

• The responsible individual or one of the partners as the case may be
• Another of the directors or other persons responsible for the management of the organisation or partnership
• An employee of the organisations or partnership not directly concerned with the conduct of the home [reg.33(2)]

■ The visits referred to above must be at least monthly and may be unannounced [reg.33(3)].

■ The person carrying out the visit must:

• Interview, with their consent and in private such of the residents, parents, relatives and persons working at the home as appears necessary to form an opinion of the standard of care provided
• Inspect the premises and records of any complaints

- Prepare a written report on the conduct of the home [reg.33(4)]

■ The registered provider must supply a copy of the above report to:

- The Chief Inspector
- Registered manager of the home and
- If the registered provider is an organisation, to each of the directors or other persons responsible for management of the organisation, and where the registered provider is a partnership, to each of the partners [reg.33(5)]

Review of Quality of Care [Reg. 34 & Sch.6 Children's Homes Regulations 2001 (as amended)]

■ The registered person must establish and maintain a system for monitoring at appropriate intervals, matters set out in Sch. 6 (reproduced below) and for improving the quality of care:

- For each resident, compliance with placing authority's plan for care of child (where applicable) and the placement plan
- Deposit and issue of money and other valuable handed in for safekeeping
- All accidents and injuries sustained in the home or by children accommodated there
- Any illness of residents
- Complaints in relation to residents and their outcomes

- Any allegations or suspicions of abuse with respect to residents and the outcome of any investigation
- Staff recruitment records and conduct of required checks for new workers in the home
- Visitors to the home and to children in the home
- Notifications of events listed in Sch. 5
- Any incident when a child accommodated in the home goes missing
- Use of measures of control, restraint and discipline in respect of children accommodated there
- Risk assessments for health and safety purposes and subsequent action taken
- Medicines, medical treatment and first aid administered to any child accommodated
- In the case of qualifying school, the standard of educational provision
- Duty rosters of persons working at the home and rosters actually worked
- Fire drills and tests of alarms and of fire equipment
- Records of appraisals of employees
- Minutes of staff meetings [reg.34(1) & Sch.6]

■ The registered person must supply to the Chief Inspector a report of any review s/he conducts and make a copy available on request to placing authorities where the placing authority is not the parent of a child accommodated in the home [reg.34(2)].

NB. The system referred to in reg.34(1) must provide for consultation with children accommodated in the home, their parents and placing authorities [reg.34(3)]

■ The registered person must ensure a copy of the Children's Homes Regulations 2001 (and any amendments to them) as well as the national minimum standards are kept in the home and made available on request to:

- Any person working in the home
- Any child accommodated in the home
- The parent of any child accommodated in the home [reg.35]

■ The registered provider must carry on the home in such a manner as is likely to ensure it will be financially viable for the purpose of achieving the aims and objectives set out in its statement of purpose [reg.36(1)].

■ The registered person must:

- Ensure that adequate accounts are maintained and kept up to date in respect of the home

- Supply a copy to the Chief Inspector at its request [reg.36(2)]
- The registered person must provide the Chief Inspector with such information as it may require for the purpose of considering financial viability of the home, including:

  - Annual certified accounts
  - A bank reference
  - Information about financing and financial resources of the home
  - If the registered provider is a company, information as to any of its associated companies
  - A certificate of insurance covering death, injury, public liability, damage or other loss [reg.36(3)]

NB. In reg.36, a company is an associated company of another if one of them has control of the other or both are under the control of the same person [reg.36(4)].

Miscellaneous [Regs. 37–43]

■ If a registered provider (who is in day to day charge) or registered manager proposes to be absent for a continuous period of 28 days or more, the registered person must give written notice to the Chief Inspector [reg.37(1)].

■ Except in an emergency, notice must be given no later than 1 month before the proposed absence, or within such shorter period as may be agreed with the Chief Inspector.

■ The notice must specify with respect to the absence:

  • Its length or expected length and reasons for it
  • Arrangements made for running the home
  • Name, address and qualifications of the person who will be responsible for the home during the absence
  • (In the case of absence of registered manager) arrangements which have been/proposed to be made for appointing another person to manage the home during the absence, including proposed date by which the appointment is to be made [req.37(2);(3)]

■ If the absence arises as a result of an emergency, the registered person must give notice of the absence within 1 week of its occurrence specifying the matters listed in bullet points above [reg.37(3)].

- If the registered provider (if s/he is in day to day charge of the home) or the registered manager has been absent from the home for a continuous period of 28 days or more and the Chief Inspector has not been given notice of the absence, the registered person must without delay give notice in writing to her/him specifying the matters listed in the bullet points above [reg.37(4)].

- The registered person must notify the Chief Inspector of the return to duty of the registered provider or (as the case may be) the registered manager not later than 7 days after the date of her/his return [reg.37(5)].

Notice of Changes [Reg. 38 Children's Homes Regulations 2001 (as amended)]

- The registered person must give written notice to the Chief Inspector as soon as practicable to do so if any of the following events take place or are proposed to take place:

  - A person other than the registered person carries on or manages the home
  - A person ceases to carry on the home
  - Where the registered provider is an individual, she changes her/his name

- Where the registered provide is a partnership, there is any change in the membership of the partnership
- Where the registered provider is an organisation the name or address of the organisations is changed, there is any change of director, manager, secretary or similar officer, there is to be any change in identity of the responsible individual
- Where the registered provider is a company, a receiver, manager, liquidator or provisional liquidator is appointed
- The premises of the home are significantly altered or extended, or additional premises are acquired [reg.38]

Appointment of Liquidators etc [Reg. 39 Children's Homes Regulations 2001 (as amended)]

■ Any person to whom reg.39 (2) applies shall-:

- Forthwith notify the Chief inspector of her/his appointment indicating the reasons for it
- Appoint a manager to take full-time day to day charge of the children's home in any case where there is no registered manager and
- Not more than 28 days after her/his appointment notify the Chief Inspector of her/his intentions regarding the future operation of the home [reg.39(1)]

■ This paragraph applies to any person appointed as:

- The receiver or manager of the property of a company or partnership which is a registered provider of a children's home;
- A liquidator or provisional liquidator of a company which is the registered provider of a children's home; or
- The trustee in bankruptcy of a registered provider of a children's home [reg.39(2)]

Death of Registered Person [Reg. 40 Children's Homes Regulations 2001 (as amended)]

- If more than 1 person is registered in respect of a home and a registered person dies, the other registered person must without delay notify the Chief Inspector in writing [reg.40(1)].

- If only 1 person is registered and s/he dies, her/his personal representative must notify the Chief Inspector in writing without delay and (within 28 days) of her/his intentions regarding future running of the home [reg.40(2)].

- The personal representative of the deceased registered provider may carry on the home without being registered for a period not exceeding 28 days or for any period (up to a maximum of 1 year) as may be determined and confirmed in writing by the Chief Inspector [reg.40(3);(4)].

  NB. In such circumstances, the personal representative must appoint a person to take full-time day to day charge during any period in which they carry on the home without being registered with respect to it [reg.40(5)].

Compliance with Regulations [Reg. 42 Children's Homes Regulations 2001 (as amended)]

■ If there is more than 1 registered person for a home, compliance by 1 registered person with anything required by these regulations is sufficient.

Application of these Regulations with Modification for Short Breaks [reg. 42A Children's Homes Regulations 2001 (as amended)]

■ In the circumstances set out in reg.42A(2), these regulations apply in relation to a child accommodated in a children's home with the modification set out in reg.42A(3) [reg.42A(1))].

■ The circumstances are that the child is not in the care of the local authority and s/he is placed in a series of short term placements within children's homes (short breaks) where:

- No single placement is intended to last more than 17 days
- At the end of each placement, the child returns to the care of the child's parent or a person who is not the child's parent but who has parental responsibility for that child and
- The short breaks do not exceed 75 days in any period of 12 months [reg.42A(2)]

■ The modifications are that regs. 15(1)(a) (promotion of contact with family/friends etc), 18(1) (promotion of educational achievement) and 20(2)(a) and (d) (registration with GP and other health and care related issues) do not apply [reg.42A(3)].

NATIONAL MINIMUM STANDARDS

Values

- The child's welfare, safety and needs should be at the centre of their care.

- Children should have an enjoyable childhood, and benefit from excellent parenting and education, enjoying a wide range of opportunities to develop their talents and skills leading to a successful adult life.

- Children are entitled to grow up in a loving environment that can meet their developmental needs.

- Every child should have his or her wishes and feelings listened to and taken into account.

- Each child should be valued as an individual and given personalised support in line with their individual needs and background in order to develop their identity, self confidence and self-worth.

- The particular needs of disabled children and children with complex needs will be fully recognised and taken into account.

- Looked after children should wherever possible maintain relationships with birth parents and their wider family.

- Children in residential children's homes should be given the opportunity for as full an experience of a supportive family environment as possible and those working in residential children's homes will be enabled to achieve this.

- Carers will be recognised as a core member of the team around the child with an important contribution to make in planning and decision making about the child.

- It is essential that staff receive relevant development opportunities in order to provide the best care for children.

- A genuine partnership between all those involved in children's homes is essential for the National Minimum Standards (NMS) to deliver the best outcomes for children: this includes the Government, local government and other statutory agencies.

Legal Status of the Standards

■ The NMS for Children's Homes are issued by the Secretary of State under s.23 of the Care Standards Act 2000. The Secretary of State will keep the standards under review and may publish amended standards as appropriate.

■ Minimum standards do not mean standardisation of provision. The standards are designed to be applicable to the wide variety of different types of children's home. They aim to enable, rather than prevent, individual providers to develop their own particular ethos and approach based on evidence that this is the most appropriate way to meet the child's needs. Many providers will aspire to exceed these standards and develop their service in order to achieve excellence.

■ The standards are issued for use by Ofsted, who take them into account in regulating children's homes. They will also be important in other ways. The standards may be used by providers and staff in self-assessment of their services; they provide a basis for the induction and training of staff; they can be used by parents children and young people as a guide to what they should expect as a minimum a provider to do, and they can provide guidance on what is required when setting up a children's home.

Structure & Approach to Inspection/ Wider Context

- The NMS for children's homes focus on delivering achievable outcomes for children.

- Each standard is preceded by a statement of the outcome to be achieved by the children's home provider. The standards are intended to be qualitative, in that they provide a tool for judging the quality of life experienced by children and young people who are looked after, but they are also designed to be measurable.

- Providers will normally show that they are meeting the headline statement of the outcome by following the standards below. However, these do not have to be followed exactly if the provider can demonstrate, and Ofsted is satisfied, that the outcomes are being met in a different way. The exception is a requirement set out in regulations in which case the regulation must be met. The standards outline in the legislation box what the regulatory requirement is which underpins the standards.

- Across all its work, Ofsted has 3 core statutory responsibilities under s.117 Education and Inspections Act 2006: to ensure that inspection supports improvement in the services Ofsted inspects and regulates; that it is centred on the needs of users; and that it promotes the effective use of resources.

- There are 4 elements to Ofsted's function as a regulator: registration; inspection; compliance; and enforcement.

- The purpose of Ofsted's inspection of social care is to assess the quality of care being provided for children, young people, and where appropriate their families. Inspection focuses on the outcomes which they are being supported to achieve. It tests compliance with the relevant regulations, and takes into account the national minimum standards.

- Following inspection, inspectors will make a number of judgements, including a judgment on the overall effectiveness of the service inspected. They will make recommendations for improvement, including any action required to ensure that provisions fully meet the national minimum standards.

- For children's homes, Ofsted will set requirements to be fulfilled in order to remedy any identified failure to meet the relevant regulations. Any identified failure in meeting the requirements of regulations may lead to consideration of enforcement action. Conditions of registration may be imposed.

Application to Short Breaks

■ Both the Children's Homes Regulations and the NMS are modified in relation to short breaks. This is in recognition that where the child receives short breaks the parents have primary responsibility for planning for their child.

■ Short break care is defined in reg.42A Children's Homes Regulations 2001 (as amended). The modifications are that regs.15(1)(a), 18(1) and 20(2)(a) and (d) and do not apply in relation to that child.

■ The following NMS do not apply in relation to short break care; standards 2.5, 2.7 and all standard 9 and 12.

■ In addition there is not a requirement for a separate placement plan for children looked after in a series of short breaks (Care Planning, Placement and Case Review (England) Regulations (2010), reg.48 (3)). For such children the short break care plan includes key elements of the placement plan. Where the NMS state 'placement plan' this will be the short break care plan in relation to children on short breaks.

NB. Unless otherwise indicated, all references to regulations in the following pages are to the Children's Homes Regulations 2001 (as amended).

CHILD FOCUSED STANDARDS

Standard 1: Child's Wishes & Feelings & Views of Those Significant to Them

Underpinning Legislation

Regulation 11: Promotion of welfare

Regulation 15: Contact and access to communications

Regulation 34: Review of quality of care

Outcome

Children know that their views, wishes and feelings are taken into account in all aspects of their care; are helped to understand why it may not be possible to act upon their wishes in all cases; and know how to obtain support and make a complaint

The views of others with an important relationship to the child are gathered and taken into account

1.1 Children's views, wishes and feelings are acted upon, in the day to day running of the home and important decisions or changes in the child's life, unless this is contrary to their interests.

1.2 Children understand how their views have been taken into account, and where significant wishes or concerns are not acted upon, they are helped to understand why.

1.3 All children communicate their views on all aspects of their care and support.

1.4 The views of the child, the child's family, social worker and IRO are sought regularly on the child's care, (unless in individual cases this is not appropriate).

1.5 Children have access to independent advice and support from adults who they can contact directly and in private about problems or concerns, which is appropriate to their age and understanding. Children know their rights to advocacy and how to access an advocate, and how to contact the children's rights director.

1.6 Children can take up issues in the most appropriate way with support, without fear that this will result in any adverse consequences. Children receive prompt feedback on any concerns or complaints raised and are kept informed of progress.

1.7 The wishes, feelings and views of children and those significant to them are taken into account in monitoring staff and developing the home.

Standard 2: Promoting Diversity, a Positive Identity & Potential Through Individualised Care

Underpinning Legislation

Regulation 11: Promotion of welfare

Regulation 20: Health needs of children

Outcome

Children develop a positive self view, emotional resilience and knowledge and understanding of their background.

2.1 Children receive personalised care that promotes all aspects of their individual identity and are each treated as an individual rather than a member of a group.

2.2 Staff support children's social and emotional development and enable children to develop emotional resilience and self-esteem.

2.3 Staff meet children's individual needs as set out in the child's placement plan where appropriate as part of the wider children's home group.

2.4 Children exercise choice in the food that they eat and are able to prepare their own meals and snacks, within the limits that a reasonable parent would set.

2.5 Children exercise choice and independence in the clothes and personal requisites that they buy and have these needs met, within the limits that a reasonable parent would set.

NB. This sub-standard is not applicable to short break placements.

2.6 Children develop skills and emotional resilience that will prepare them for independent living.

2.7 Children receive a personal allowance appropriate to their age and understanding that is consistent with their placement plan.

NB. This sub-standard is not applicable to short break placements.

Standard 3: Promoting Positive Behaviour & Relationships

Underpinning Legislation

Regulation 17: Behaviour management, discipline and restraint

Outcome

Children enjoy sound relationships, interact positively with others and behave appropriately

3.1 The home has high expectations of all children and staff.

3.2 There is an environment and culture, which is underpinned by a clear strategy, that promotes and models and supports positive behaviour that all staff understand and implement.

3.3 The home has a clear written policy on managing behaviour, which includes supporting positive behaviour, de-escalation of conflicts, discipline, control and restraint, that all staff understand and apply at all times.

3.4 All staff understand, share and implement the home's ethos, philosophy and approach to caring for children.

3.5 Children develop and practice skills to build and maintain positive relationships, be assertive and resolve conflicts positively.

3.6 Children are encouraged to take responsibility for their behaviour, in a way that is appropriate to their age and abilities.

3.7 Each home meets children's emotional and behavioural needs, as set out in their care plan. Children's privacy and confidentiality are appropriately protected.

3.8 Sanctions and rewards for behaviour are clear, reasonable and fair and are understood by all staff and children;

3.9 Staff understand, and manage their own feelings and responses to the emotions and behaviours presented by children and understand how past experiences and present emotions are communicated through behaviour.

3.10 Staff are supported to manage their responses and feelings arising from working with children, particularly where children display challenging behaviour or have difficult emotional issues. Staff are supported to understand how children's previous experiences can manifest in challenging behaviour;

3.11 Children do not identify bullying as a problem at the home. Staff and children understand bullying is unacceptable. Staff working in the home understand their role in helping to prevent and counter bullying by any adult or child living or working in the home;

3.12 Staff in the home are trained to recognise and deal with any indications or incidents of bullying, to act proactively and intervene positively, engaging with those who bully as well as those who are bullied.

3.13 Methods to de-escalate confrontations or potentially violent behaviour are used wherever appropriate to avoid use of physical restraint. Restraint is only used in exceptionally unusual circumstances, to prevent injury to any person including the child being restrained or to prevent serious damage to the property of any person including the child being restrained. In a secure children's home restraint may be used for the purpose of preventing a child from absconding.

3.14 Restraint is not used as a punishment, nor to force compliance with instructions where significant harm or serious damage to property are not otherwise likely. Use of restraint is set out in the home's behaviour management policy and is in line with any relevant government guidance on approved approaches to restraint.

3.15 Where children's homes use restraint, staff are trained in the use of physical restraint techniques and only use the home's agreed techniques. Training is regularly refreshed.

3.16 Where there has been physical restraint, children are always given the opportunity to be examined by a registered nurse or medical practitioner. Homes must be able to call on medical assistance as required.

3.17 All children and staff are given an opportunity to discuss incidents of restraint they have been involved in, witnessed or been affected by, with a relevant adult.

3.18 Where any sanctions, disciplinary measures or restraint are used, children are encouraged to have their views recorded in the records kept by the home.

3.19 No children's home restricts the liberty of any child as a matter of routine or provides any form of secure accommodation unless that home is an approved secure children's home.

3.20 Each home only carries out searches of a child, their room or their possessions in accordance with the homes guidance.

3.21 Each home regularly reviews incidents of challenging behaviour, examines trends or issues emerging from this, to enable staff to reflect and learn to inform future practice.

3.22 The home's approach to care minimises the need for police involvement to deal with challenging behaviour and avoids criminalising children unnecessarily. The home follows procedures and guidance on police involvement in the home, which has been agreed with local police.

Standard 4: Safeguarding Children

Underpinning Legislation

Regulation 16: Arrangements for the protection of children

Outcome

Children feel safe and are safe. Children understand how to protect themselves; and feel protected and are protected from significant harm including neglect, abuse, and accident

4.1 Children's safety and welfare is promoted in the home. Children are protected from abuse and other forms of significant harm (including sexual or labour exploitation).

4.2 Staff actively and promote the welfare of children living in the home.

4.3 Staff make positive relationships with children in the home, generate a culture of openness and trust and are aware of and alert to any signs or symptoms that might indicate that a child is at risk of harm.

4.4 Staff encourage children to take appropriate risks as a normal part of growing up. Children are helped to understand how to keep themselves safe including when outside the home when using the internet or social media.

4.5 The home implements a proportionate approach to any risk assessment.

4.6 Staff are trained in appropriate safer-care practice, including skills to care for children who have been abused. For providers who offer placements to disabled children, this includes training specifically on issues affecting disabled children.

4.7 The registered person and staff work effectively in partnership with other agencies concerned with child protection e.g. the responsible authority, schools, hospitals, general practitioners, etc and do not work in isolation from them.

4.8 Unchecked visitors are adequately 'chaperoned' when on the home's premises.

Standard 5: Children Missing from Care

Underpinning Legislation

Regulation 16: Arrangements for the protection of children

Regulation 30: Notifiable events + Schedule 5 (events and notifications)

Outcome

Children rarely go missing and if they do, they return quickly

Children who do go missing are protected as far as possible and responded to positively on their return

5.1 The care and support provided to children minimises the risk that they will go missing and reduces the risk of harm should the child go missing.

5.2 Staff working within the home know and implement the local authority and home's policy in relation to children going missing and their role in implementing that policy.

5.3 Staff are aware of and do not exceed, the measures they can take to prevent a child leaving without permission under current legislation and government guidance.

5.4 Children who are absent from the home without consent but whose whereabouts are known or thought to be known by staff are protected in line with the home's written procedure.

5.5 Staff actively search for children who are missing, including working with police where appropriate.

5.6 If a child is absent from the home and their whereabouts is not known (i.e. the child is missing), the home's procedures are compatible with the local Runaway and Missing from Home and Care (RMFHC) protocols and procedures applicable to the area where the home is located.

5.7 Where children placed out of authority go missing, the registered manager of the home follows the local RMFHC protocol, complies with and makes staff aware of any other processes required by the placing authority, specified in the individual child's care plan and in the RMFHC protocol covering the authority responsible for the child's care.

5.8 Children are helped to understand the dangers and risks of leaving the home without permission and are made aware of where they can access help if they consider running away.

5.9 Where a child goes missing and there is concern for their welfare, or at the request of a child who has been missing, staff arrange a meeting between the child and the responsible authority in private to consider the reasons for the child going missing. The home considers with the responsible authority what action should be taken to prevent the child going missing in future. Any concerns arising about the placement are addressed, as far as possible, in conjunction with the responsible authority.

5.10 Written records kept by the home when a child goes missing detail action taken by staff, the circumstances of the child's return, any reasons given by the child for running away from the home, and any action taken in the light of those reasons. This information is shared with the responsible authority and where appropriate, their parents.

Standard 6: Promoting Good Health & Wellbeing

Underpinning Legislation

Regulation 20: Health needs of children

Regulation 21: Medicines

Outcome

Children live in a healthy environment where their physical, emotional and psychological health is promoted and where they are able to access the services to meet their health needs

6.1   Children's physical and emotional and social development needs are promoted.

6.2   Children understand their health needs, how to maintain a healthy lifestyle and to make informed decisions about their own health.

6.3   Children are encouraged to participate in a range of positive activities that contribute to their physical and emotional health.

6.4   Children have prompt access to doctors and other health professionals, including specialist services, when they need these services.

6.5   Children's health is promoted in accordance with their placement plan and staff are clear about what responsibilities and decisions are delegated to them and where consent for medical treatment needs to be obtained.

6.6   Children's wishes and feelings are sought and taken into account in their health care, according to their understanding, and staff advocate on behalf of children.

6.7   Staff have received sufficient training on health and hygiene issues and first aid with particular emphasis on health promotion and communicable diseases.

6.8   Staff receive guidance and training to provide appropriate care if looking after children with complex health needs

6.9   The home has good links with health agencies, including specialist services where appropriate, such as CAMHS and sexual health services. The availability of such services is taken into account when deciding on admissions.

6.10   Staff involved in delivering therapeutic interventions have appropriate training and expertise and access to regular supervision.

6.11   Specific therapies are used only:

    a.   where there is a clear and widely accepted theoretical or evidence base underpinning its effectiveness

    b.   with the continuing agreement of the child's responsible authority or a person with

parental responsibility and of the child
concerned where the child is of sufficient
understanding

6.12 Each child's wishes and feelings are sought and
taken into account in their health care, according to
their understanding, and each has someone in the
home who can advocate these for them.

6.13 Medicines which are kept in the home are stored
safely and are accessible only by those for whom
they are intended.

6.14 Prescribed medication is only given to the child for
whom it was prescribed, and in accordance with the
prescription. Children who are able and wish to
keep and take their own medication, can do so
safely.

6.15 There is a written record of all medication,
treatment and first aid given to children during
their placement.

6.16 The home has any physical adaptations or
equipment needed to provide appropriate care for
children.

Standard 7: Leisure Activities

Underpinning Legislation

Regulation: 18: Education, employment and leisure activity

Outcome

Children are able to enjoy their interests, develop confidence in their skills and are supported and encouraged by staff to engage in leisure activities

Children are able to make a positive contribution to their home and their wider community

7.1 Children develop their emotional, intellectual, social creative and physical skills through the accessible and stimulating environment created by the home. Children are supported to take part in school based and out of school activities.

7.2 Children pursue individual interests and hobbies. This includes taking part in a range of activities, including leisure activities and trips.

7.3 Staff understand what is in the child's placement plan and have clarity about decisions they can make about the day to day arrangements for the child, including such matters as education, leisure activities, overnight stays, holidays, and personal issues such as hair cuts.

7.4 Staff are supported to make reasonable and appropriate decisions within the authority delegated to them, without having to seek consent unnecessarily.

7.5 Children take part in age appropriate peer activities as would normally be granted by the parent to their children and within the framework of the placement plan, decision-making and any assessment of risk to the child should be undertaken on the same basis as a reasonable parent would do

7.6 Children are encouraged and enabled to make and sustain friendships with children outside the home, which may involve friends visiting the home and reciprocal arrangements to visit friends' homes.

7.7 Children can stay overnight with friends if staff consider it appropriate in individual circumstances and subject to the requirements of care or placement plans, without a requirement that friends' parents should be police or CRB checked.

Standard 8: Promoting Educational Achievement

Underpinning Legislation

Regulation 18 – Education, employment and leisure activity

Outcome

The education and achievement of children is actively promoted as valuable in itself and as part of their preparation for adulthood. Children are supported to achieve their educational potential

8.1 Children, including pre-school and older children have a home which promotes a learning environment and supports their development.

8.2 Children have access to a range of educational resources to support their learning and have opportunities beyond the school day to engage in activities which promote learning.

8.3 Children are supported to attend school or alternative provision regularly.

8.4 Children are helped by staff to achieve their educational or training goals. This includes providing support, facilities and opportunities as needed. Staff work with a child's education provider to maximise each child's achievement and to minimise any underachievement.

8.5 Each home has and is fully implementing, a written education policy that promotes a culture that values children's education.

8.6 The home maintains regular contact with each child's school and other education settings, with staff attending all parents' meetings as appropriate. Staff advocate for the child where appropriate.

8.7 Staff engage and work with schools, colleges, other organisations, and the placing local authority to support children's education including advocating to help overcome any problems the child may be experiencing in their education setting. Staff have up-to-date information about each child's educational progress and school attendance record.

8.8 Children who have been excluded from school have access to appropriate education and training.

8.9 If children no longer receive compulsory full time education, when appropriate the home supports them to participate in further education, training or employment.

Standard 9: Promoting & Supporting Contact

Underpinning Legislation

Regulation 15: Contact and access to communications

Outcome

Children have, where appropriate, constructive contact with their parents, grandparents, siblings, half-siblings, families, friends and other people who play a significant role in their lives

9.1 Children are supported and encouraged to maintain and develop family contacts and friendships, subject to any limitations or provisions set out in their care plan, placement plan and any court order. Appropriate forms of contact are promoted and facilitated for each child, including where appropriate visits to the child in the home, visits by the child to relatives or friends, meetings with relatives or friends, letters, exchange of photographs and electronic forms of contact.

9.2 Staff have appropriate training, supervision and support if they are required to supervise and facilitate contact.

9.3 Emergency restrictions on contact are only made to protect the child from significant risk to their safety or welfare and are communicated to the responsible authority within 24 hours of being imposed.

9.4 Ongoing restriction on communication by the child is agreed by the child's responsible authority, takes the child's wishes and feelings into account and is regularly reviewed in collaboration with the responsible authority.

9.5 The home feeds back to the responsible authority any significant reactions a child has to contact arrangements or visits with any person.

9.6 When deciding whether to offer a placement, the registered person works with the responsible authority in giving consideration to how the child's contact with family and significant others will be supported, particularly where a child is placed at a distance from home.

9.7 Staff understand what decisions about contact are delegated to them, in line with the child's care plan, and make those decisions in the child's best interests.

NB. The above standards are not required for short breaks. For children in short breaks the responsible person must know how to contact parents if necessary and maintain such contact as has been agreed in the short break care plan.

Standard 10: Providing a Suitable Physical Environment for the Child

Underpinning Legislation

Regulation 31: Fitness of premises

Outcome

Children live in well designed, safe and pleasant homes with adequate space in a suitable location where there is access to the necessary facilities for a range of activities which will promote their development

10.1 Each home is situated in a location that supports its aims and objectives and proposed models of care for children and young people. This includes children being able to access external services, recreational activities and to maintain and develop relationships with family and friends.

10.2 The home's location and design promotes children's health, safety and well-being and avoids factors such as excessive isolation and areas that present significant risks to children.

10.3 The home provides a comfortable and homely environment and is well maintained and decorated. Avoidable hazards are removed as is consistent with a domestic setting. Risk reduction does not lead to an institutional feel.

10.4 Physical restrictions on normal movement within or from the home are not used unless this is necessary to safeguard children and promote their welfare and development. Such measures are only used where agreed with the responsible authority and, if appropriate, the parents. Such restrictions for one child do not impose similar restrictions on other children.

10.5 For children's homes that are not secure children's homes where specific measures, including electronic devices, are used to monitor children, there is a written policy that sets out how they should be used, how they promote the welfare of children, how children will be informed of their use, how legitimate privacy of children will be protected and how children will be protected from potential abuse of such measures.

10.6 Secure children's homes have emergency call systems that are effective in summoning staff assistance when needed.

10.7 Staff preparation and training cover health and safety issues. Staff are provided with written guidelines on their health and safety responsibilities. Where homes offer placements for disabled children, the accommodation must be suitable to the particular needs of disabled children which may include suitable aids, adaptations and other suitable equipment.

10.8 Risk assessments of the whole children's home environment are carried out, recorded in writing and regularly reviewed.

10.9 There is an emergency escape plan that all staff and children are familiar with and have practiced so they know what to do in an emergency;

10.10 Each child has their own bedroom. If this is not possible, no more than two children share a room in a home that is not a school. In those homes that are schools, there are no more than four children of a similar age or stage per bedroom, and each child has a personal area.

10.11 Bedrooms are not shared unless each child freely agrees to the arrangement, and are not shared by children of different genders, or children of significantly different ages (other than siblings where this is appropriate). The choice of whether a child has a separate room or shares is made only after careful consideration of all available facts including the risk of bullying or abuse.

10.12 A request by a child to change bedrooms is given urgent consideration and agreed if feasible.

10.13 Children accommodated in emergency provision (subject to a home's Statement of Purpose allowing such a placement) are not placed in a shared bedroom (other than with siblings) until an assessment has been carried out to ascertain their views and the views of those who already sleep in the bedroom.

10.14 Bedrooms are not shared between children and staff or adult visitors.

Standard 11: Preparation for a Placement

Underpinning Legislation

Care, Planning, Placement and Case Review (England) Regulations (2010)

Outcome

Children are welcomed into the home and leave the home in a planned and appropriate manner which makes them feel valued

11.1 Each home has and implements clear procedures for introducing children to the home, the staff and the other children living there, which covers planned and where permitted, emergency/ immediate placements. They help children understand what to expect from living in the home.

11.2 The children's home only provides admission to children whose assessed needs they can reasonably expect to meet.

11.3 Unless an emergency placement makes it impossible, children are given information before arrival about the home and any other information they need or reasonably request about the placement, in a format appropriate to their age and understanding, including photographs where appropriate. Wherever possible, children are able to visit the home prior to a placement decision being made. Children can bring their favourite possessions into the home.

11.4 The home does not operate in a way which increases the risk of separation of siblings.

11.5 Each child can remain in the home until moving on is in their best interests (taking their wishes and feelings into account) unless this is impracticable or is against the welfare of others.

11.6 A review must take place before a child is moved to another placement, except in an emergency. If a placement move occurs in an emergency, the responsible authority is informed within 1 working day.

11.7 The registered person does not admit children in an emergency unless explicitly included as a function of the home and the home is at the time of admission able to provide a bedroom and appropriate facilities. A review is initiated no more than 72 hours after any emergency admission to consider whether the child should remain at the home, or it is in that child's interests to move to a different placement.

11.8 Where children are leaving the home, they are helped to understand the reasons why they are leaving. Children are supported during the transition to their new placement, to independent living or to their parental home

Standard 12: Promoting Independence & Moves to Adulthood & leaving Care

Underpinning Legislation

Regulation 11: Promotion of welfare

Children Act 1989 – Ss. 22, 61 & 64

Outcome

Children receive care which helps to prepare them for, and support them into, adulthood so that they can reach their potential and achieve economic wellbeing

12.1 Children are supported to:

a. establish positive and appropriate social and sexual relationships

b. develop positive self-esteem

c. prepare for the world of work and or further or higher education

d. prepare for moving into their own accommodation

e. develop practical skills, including shopping, buying, cooking and keeping food, washing clothes, personal self-care, and understanding and taking responsibility for personal healthcare

f.   develop financial capability, knowledge and skills

g.   know about entitlements to financial and other support after leaving care, including benefits and support from social care services

12.2 The home contributes to the development of each child's care plan, including the pathway plan for 'eligible' care leavers and works collaboratively with the young person's social worker or personal adviser in implementing the plan.

12.3 The home liaises with the child's responsible authority and their IRO where applicable, about the progress of the child's readiness to move to any future accommodation where they would expect to take on greater responsibility and personal independence.

12.4 Homes support the young person's transition to adult services, when required by the care plan.

NB. The above standards are not required for short breaks.

STANDARDS OF THE CHILDREN'S HOME PROVIDER

Standard 13: Statement of Purpose & Children's Guide

Underpinning Legislation

Regulation 4: Statement of purpose and children's guide

Regulation 5: Review of statement of purpose and children's guide

Outcome

Children, staff and the placing authority are clear about the aim's and objectives of the home and what services and facilities it provides

The provider meets the aims and objectives in the statement of purpose

13.1 The children's home has a clear statement of purpose which is available to and understood by staff and children and reflected in any policies, procedures and guidance. It is available to the responsible authority and any parent or person with parental responsibility.

13.2 The aims and objectives of the statement of purpose are child focused and show how the service will meet outcomes for children.

13.3 The registered person approves the statement of purpose and the children's guide and reviews them at least annually.

13.4 Subject to the child's age and understanding, the children's home ensures the child receives the children's guide at the point of placement and that the contents of the children's guide is explained to the child in a way that is accessible.

13.5 The guide includes a summary of what the home sets out to do for children, how they can find out their rights, how a child can contact their IRO, children's rights director, Ofsted if they wish to raise a concern with inspectors, and how to secure access to an independent advocate.

13.6 Where a child requires it the guide is available when appropriate through suitable alternative methods of communication, e.g. Makaton, pictures, tape recording, translation into another language.

Standard 14: Fitness to Provide or Manage the Administration of a Children's Home

Underpinning Legislation

Regulation 6: Fitness of registered provider

Regulation 7: Appointment of manager

Regulation 8: Fitness of manager

Regulation 9: Registered person – general requirements
Regulation 36: Financial position

Outcome

The home is provided and managed by those who are suitable to work with children and have the appropriate skills, experience and qualifications to deliver an efficient and effective service

14.1 The registered provider and registered manager of the home:

   a.   have good knowledge and experience of law and practice relating to looked after children
   b.   have business and management skills to manage the work efficiently and effectively and
   c.   have financial expertise to ensure the home is run on a sound financial basis including long-term financial viability of the home.

14.2 The registered manager (or registered person, where
the registered person is an individual and there is
no registered manager) has:

a.   a recognised social work qualification or a
professional qualification relevant to working
with children at least at level 4

b.   a qualification in management at least at
level 4*

c.   at least 2 years experience relevant to
residential care within the last 5 years; and

d.   at least 1 years experience supervising and
managing professional staff

14.3 Appointees to the role of registered manager who
do not have the management qualification (above)
must enrol on a management training course within
6 months, and obtain a relevant management
qualification within 3 years, of their appointment.

14.4 The responsibilities and duties of the registered
manager and to whom they are accountable are
clear and understood by the manager. The manager
is notified in writing of any changes the person to
whom accountable

---

* With respect to standard 14.2 (a) and (b), for persons under-
taking a qualification after January 2011, the relevant qualification will be the Level 5 Diploma in Leadership for Health and
Social Care and Children and Young People's Services. Managers
who already hold a Level 4 Leadership and Management for
Care Service and Health and Social Care will not need to undertake this qualification at level 5.

14.5 The registered manager exercises effective leadership of the home's staff and operation, such that the home is organised, managed and staffed in a manner that delivers sound, good quality care meeting the individual needs of each child at the home.

Standard 15: Financial Viability & Changes Affecting Business Continuity

Underpinning Legislation

Regulation 36: Financial position

Regulation 39: Appointment of liquidators

Outcome

The provider is financially sound

Where a service is to close or substantially change, there is proper planning to make the transition for children, carers and staff as smooth as possible

15.1 A qualified accountant certifies the annual accounts demonstrate that the home is financially viable and likely to have sufficient funding to continue to fulfil its statement of purpose for at least the next 12 months.

15.2 The registered person has a written development plan, reviewed annually, for the future of the home, either identifying any planned changes in the operation or resources of the service, or confirming the continuation of the home's current operation and resource.

15.3 Where the home, for financial, staffing or other reasons, cannot adequately and consistently maintain provision which complies with regulations or national minimum standards, an effective plan must be established and implemented either to rectify the situation or to close down the service.

15.4 The registered person must notify Ofsted, all current responsible authorities and the area authority if closure of the home or substantial change to the home significantly affecting the care, welfare or placement of children, is likely or is actively being considered. The registered person should work with the responsible authority and area authority to ensure as smooth a transition for children and staff as possible.

15.5 Confidential records of a home that closes must be passed to a statutory authority or organisation for safe keeping and for future access by children in accordance with legal requirements.

15.6 Any person or organisation temporarily responsible for a home in administration or receivership, or in the process of closure or substantial change, must operate the service in the best interests of the placed children under the circumstances that apply, in accordance with the applicable these standards.

Standard 16: Suitability to Work with Children

Underpinning Legislation

Regulation 16: Arrangements for the protection of children

Regulation 26: Fitness of workers

Regulation 27: Employment of staff

Outcome

There is careful selection and vetting of staff and volunteers working with children in the home and there is monitoring of such people to help prevent unsuitable people from having the opportunity to harm children.

16.1 All people working in or for the children's home are interviewed as part of the selection process and have references checked to assess suitability before taking on responsibilities. Telephone enquiries are made as well as obtaining written references .

16.2 The registered person can demonstrate, including from written records, that it consistently follows good recruitment practice, and all applicable current statutory requirements and guidance, in staff recruitment and carers selection. This includes CRB checks and, once the relevant legislation is in force, verifying that a person is subject to monitoring, under the Vetting and Barring Scheme . All personnel responsible for recruitment and selection of staff are trained in, understand and operate these good practices.

16.3 The children's home has a record of the recruitment and vetting checks which have been carried out on those working (including as volunteers) for the children's home which includes:

a. identity checks

b. CRB Disclosures, including the level of the disclosure, the unique reference number, and the outcome of the check including whether the individual is barred (in line with eligibility to obtain such checks)

c. checks to confirm qualifications which are a requirement and those that are considered by the children's home to be relevant

d. at least 2 references, preferably 1 from a current employer and, where possible, a statement from each referee as to their opinion of the person's suitability to work with children

e. checks to confirm the right to work in the UK; and

f. where the person has lived outside of the UK, further checks as are considered appropriate where obtaining a CRB disclosure is not sufficient to establish suitability to work with children

16.4 The record must show the date on which each check was completed who carried out the check. The CRB disclosure information must be kept in secure conditions and be destroyed by secure means as soon as it is no longer needed. Before the disclosure is destroyed, records need to be kept as described above.

16.5 The registered person's system for recruiting staff and others includes an effective system for reaching decisions as to who is to be appointed and the circumstances in which an application should be refused in relation to staff or others, in the light of any criminal convictions or other concerns about suitability that are declared or discovered through the recruitment process.

16.6 Staff members and others subject to the above checks do not normally start work at the home until all the checks required in the Children's Homes Regulations are completed.

16.7 There is a whistle-blowing policy which is made known to all staff and volunteers. This makes it a clear duty for such people to report to an appropriate authority any circumstances within the home which they consider likely to significantly harm the safety, rights or welfare of any child at the home.

16.8 Where practicable, children are involved in the recruitment of staff of the home.

Standard 17: Sufficient Staffing of the Home

Underpinning Legislation

Regulation 25: Staffing of Children's Homes

Outcome

Staff are sufficient in experience, qualification and number to meet the needs of the children

17.1 The overall competence of staff and number and deployment of staff, both as a staff group and on individual shifts, can fulfil the home's statement of purpose and meet individual needs of all children resident in the home.

17.2 Records of staff working in the home demonstrate the staffing level.

17.3 Contingency plans are in place in the event of a shortfall in staffing levels

17.4 There are clear arrangements for staff to deputise in the registered person's absence and the deputy to the registered person of the home (or the person designated to deputise for the registered person in her/his absence) has at least 1 year's relevant supervisory experience.

17.5 Staff members who are placed in charge of the home and other staff at particular times (e.g. as leaders of staff shifts) have substantial relevant experience of working in the home and have successfully completed their induction and probationary periods.

17.6 Staff rotas have time scheduled to ensure handovers are held and that they include the planning of spending time with individual children.

17.7 The registered person has in place a staff disciplinary procedure which is clear. The procedure clearly separates staff disciplinary processes from child protection enquiries and criminal proceedings, and is known by staff.

17.8 The registered person makes every effort to achieve continuity of staffing such that children's attachments are not overly disrupted. No more than half the staff on duty at any one time, by day or night, at the home are to be from an external agency, and no member of staff from an external agency is to be alone on duty at night in the home.

17.9 Where only 1 member of staff is on duty at any time, a risk assessment has been carried out and recorded in writing, identifying any likely risks to children, staff and members of the public.

17.10 The staff group in day- to- day contact with children includes staff of both genders whenever possible. Where the home's Statement of Purpose makes it explicit that the home uses staff of one gender only, clear guidance is provided and implemented on how children are enabled to maintain relationships with members of the opposite gender to the staff group. Staffing arrangements also take into consideration children's ethnic and cultural backgrounds and any disabilities they may have.

17.11 All care staff are at least 18 years old, and staff who are given sole responsibility for children or a management role are at least 21 years old. Within this requirement no person works in a children's home unless they are at least 4 years older than the oldest child accommodated.

17.12 Staff and residents know who is sleeping in the home each night.

Standard 18: Training, Development & Qualification of Staff

Underpinning Legislation

Regulation 25: Staffing of children's homes

Regulation 27: Employment of staff

Outcome

Children are looked after by staff who are trained and competent to meet their needs

Staff receive high quality training to enhance their individual skills and to keep them up-to-date with professional and legal developments

18.1 There is a good quality learning and development programme which staff and volunteers are supported to undertake. It includes induction, post-qualifying and in-service training to enhance individual skills and to keep staff up-to-date with professional and legal developments. Staff are equipped with the skills required to meet the needs of the children and purpose of the setting, and training keeps them up-to-date with professional, legal and practice developments and reflects the policies, legal obligations and business needs of the home.

18.2 The learning and development program is evaluated for effectiveness at least annually and if necessary is updated.

18.3 New staff, undertake the Children's Workforce Development Council's induction standards, commencing within 7 working days of starting their employment and being completed within 6 months.

18.4 All social workers and other specialist professionals (e.g. medical, legal, educationalists, psychologists, therapists) are professionally qualified and, where applicable, registered by the appropriate professional body. They are appropriately trained to work with children and their families, and have a good understanding of residential child care and the policies and purpose of the home.

18.5 All existing care staff have attained a minimum level 3 qualification[†]. All new staff engaged from the commencement of the NMS (in April 2011) to hold level 3 Children & Young Peoples Workforce Diploma which must include mandatory social care units; or be working towards the Diploma within 6 months of confirmation of employment.

[†] Previously NVQ caring for children & young people or NVQ health & social care. From September 2010 Children & Young Peoples Workforce Diploma

Standard 19: Staff Support & Supervision

Underpinning Legislation

Regulation 27: Employment of staff

Outcome

Staff and volunteers are supported and guided to fulfil their roles and provide a high quality service to children

19.1 The employer is fair and competent, and operates sound employment practices and good support for its staff and volunteers.

19.2 All staff, volunteers and the registered person, are properly managed, supported and understand to whom they are accountable.

19.3 Suitable arrangements exist for professional supervision of the registered person of the agency.

19.4 Staff have access to support and advice, and are provided with regular supervision by appropriately qualified and experienced staff.

19.5 A written record is kept by the home detailing the time and date and length of each supervision held for each member of staff, including the registered person. The record is signed by the supervisor and the member of staff at the end of the supervision.

19.6 All staff have their performance individually and formally appraised at least annually and this appraisal takes into account any views of children the service is providing for.

19.7 Staff and volunteers are easily able to access the advice needed to provide a comprehensive service for children and young people.

Standard 20: Handling Allegations & Suspicions of Harm

Underpinning Legislation

Regulation 16: Arrangements for the protection of children

Outcome

Investigations into allegations or suspicions of harm are handled fairly, quickly, and consistently in a way that provides effective protection for children, the person making the allegation, and at the same time supports the person who is the subject of the allegation

20.1 All staff and volunteers understand what they must do if they receive an allegation or have suspicions that a person may have:

    a.   behaved in a way that has, or may have, harmed a child

    b.   possibly committed a criminal offence against or related to a child or

    c.   behaved towards a child in a way that indicates he or she is unsuitable to work with children

The children's home ensures that the required actions are taken, or have been taken, in any relevant situation of which it is aware.

20.2 The children's home procedure is in line with Government guidance and requirements including the duty to refer information to statutory bodies. It is known to staff, volunteers and children.

20.3 The home's protection procedures and how staff will be supported should there be an allegation are made available to staff and volunteers. The provider takes any comments on these procedures into account.

20.4 The provider's child protection procedures are submitted for consideration and comment to the Local Safeguarding Children Board (LSCB) and to the Local Authority Designated Officer (LADO) for Child Protection[†] (or other senior officer responsible for child protection matters in that department) and are consistent with the local policies and procedures agreed by the LSCB relevant to the geographical area of the home. Any conflicts between locally agreed procedures and those of other responsible authorities are discussed and resolved as far as possible.

20.5 The children's home has a designated person, who is a senior manager, responsible for managing allegations. This designated person has responsibility for liaising with the local authority designated officer (LADO) and for keeping the subject of the allegation informed of progress during and after the investigation.

[†] See the referrals page of www.isa-gov.org.uk for information on the legal requirements for making referrals

20.6 Allegations against people that work with children are reported by the designated person to the LADO. This includes allegations that on the face of it may appear relatively insignificant or that have also been reported directly to the police or Children and Family Services.

20.7 A clear and comprehensive summary of any allegations made against a particular member of staff, including details of how the allegation was followed up and resolved, a record of any action taken and the decisions reached, is kept on the person's confidential file and a copy is provided to the person as soon as the investigation is concluded. The information is retained on the confidential file, even after someone leaves the organisation, until the person reaches normal retirement age, or for 10 years if this is longer.

20.8 Investigations into allegations or suspicions of harm are handled fairly, quickly, and consistently in a way that provides effective protection for the child, and at the same time supports the person who is the subject of the allegation. Providers follow the framework for managing cases of allegations of abuse against people who work with children as set out in *Working Together to Safeguard Children*. (revised in March 2010).

Standard 21: Managing Effectively & Efficiently & Monitoring the Home

Underpinning Legislation

Regulation 34: Review of quality of care

Regulation 33: Visits by the registered provider

Regulation 37: Notice of absence

Regulation 38: Notice of changes

Outcome

The Children's Home is managed ethically, effectively and efficiently, delivering a service which meets the needs of its users.

The registered person monitors the welfare of the children the service provides for including consultation with children about their welfare

21.1 There are clear and effective procedures for monitoring and controlling the activities of the home. This includes the financial viability of the home, any serious incidents, allegations, complaints about the provision, and the quality of the provision. Children in the home are regularly involved in contributing to monitoring the operation of the home, and their views and any concerns are seriously taken into account.

21.2 The manager regularly monitors, in line with regulations, all records kept by the home to ensure compliance with the homes policies, to identify any concerns about specific incidents and to identify patterns and trends. Immediate action is taken to address any issues raised by this monitoring.

21.3 Management of the home ensures all staff's work is consistent with these Regulations and National Minimum Standards the homes policies and procedures.

21.4 Managers and staff are clear about their roles and responsibilities. The level of delegation and responsibility of the manager and staff, and the lines of accountability, are clearly defined.

21.5 Clear arrangements are in place to ensure appropriate management of the home when the registered manager is absent.

21.6 The registered person ensures copies of inspection reports by Ofsted are available to all members of staff, children living in the home, and the children's parents/carers and on request to responsible authorities of children living in the home or those considering placing a child in the home.

21.7 Visits of the home carried out under regulation 33 include relevant checks set out in regulations and checks of any disciplinary measures and use of restraint.

21.8   The registered provider's written report of a visit carried out under regulation 33 visit is lodged in the home for the manager and staff to read and to respond.

21.9   The registered person takes action to address any issues of concern that they identify or which is raised with them.

21.10 The registered person has provided the home with a written procedure for considering complaints and responding to representations and complaints in accordance with legal requirements and relevant statutory guidance.

Standard 22: Records

Underpinning Legislation

Regulation 28: Children's case records

Regulation 29: Other records

Outcome

Records are clear, up to date and stored securely, and contribute to an understanding of the child's life

22.1 The home has and implements a written policy that clarifies the purpose, format and content of information to be kept on the registered person's files and information to be kept on the child's files. Staff understand the nature of records maintained and follow the home's policy for the keeping and retention of files, managing confidential information, and access to files (including files removed from the premises). There is a system in place to monitor the quality and adequacy of record keeping and take action when needed.

22.2 Children and their parents understand the nature of records maintained and how to access them.

22.3 Information about individual children is kept confidential and only shared with those who have a legitimate need to know the information.

22.4 Entries in records are legible, clearly expressed, non-stigmatising and distinguish as far as possible between fact, opinion and third party information.

22.5 Information about the child is recorded clearly and in a way which will be helpful to the child when they access their files now or in the future. Children are actively encouraged to read their files, confidential or third party information and to correct errors and add personal statements.

22.6 Staff support and encourage the child to reflect on and understand their history, according to their age and understanding, and to keep appropriate memorabilia of their time in the placement. Staff record and help children make a record of (subject to age and understanding), significant life events.

22.7 The registered person works with the responsible authority to ensure effective sharing of information held in the home's records about the child and information held in the responsible authorities records. The registered person provides copies of the records and documents in relation to children placed by the responsible authority immediately, on receipt of a written request.

Standard 23: Secure Accommodation & Refuges

Underpinning Legislation

Refuges: S.51 Children Act 1989

Secure Children's Homes: The Children (Secure Accommodation) Regulations 1991

Outcome

Children living in a secure children's home or refuges experience positive support with their problems as well as security or refuge, and receive the same measures to safeguard and promote their rights and welfare as they should in other children's homes

23.1 Apart from the measures essential to the home's status as a secure children's home or refuge, children resident in secure units or approved refuges receive the same care services, rights and protections as they should in other children's homes.

23.2 Staff are trained in resettlement issues in order to prepare young people effectively for leaving the secure children's home or refuge.

23.3 The secure children's home has clear and appropriate policies and practice agreed with the LSCB which effectively safeguard children from harm e.g. regular security searches of communal areas to reduce likelihood of potentially dangerous items. Such policies are reviewed in light of any serious incidents.

23.4 Secure children's homes have explicit policies and procedures that effectively identify and counter risks of self harm and suicide. Staff understand their responsibilities under these policies so that children are safeguarded.'

23.5 Surveillance is no more restrictive than necessary, having regard to the child's need for privacy.

23.6 CCTV is used in communal areas to contribute to the protection of young people from bullying, abuse or malicious allegations. The home has a written policy on the use of CCTV including how it will be used to safeguard children and protect staff.

23.7 In secure children's homes any CCTV records of any use of restraint, episode of bullying, or incident leading to a significant allegation by a young person against another young person or member of staff are reviewed by representatives of the authority responsible for the establishment and appropriate action taken.

23.8 Any secure transportation arrangements made by the home are appropriate for the secure transportation of vulnerable children.

23.9 The Chief Inspector and the responsible authority are notified promptly if a young person goes missing from the home or from an appointment or journey outside the establishment.

23.10 Young people in secure children's home only exceptionally wear special clothing to protect them against self-harm following a risk assessment. Any special clothing preserves the child's privacy and dignity.

23.11 Children are provided with appropriate education while in the home.

23.12 Observation of young people in secure children's homes does not remove reasonable privacy, and allows reasonable personal privacy during dressing, washing and using the toilet. A record is kept of all observations in bedrooms.

23.13 Young people in secure units are only placed in single separation when necessary to prevent likely serious harm to the child or others, or likely and imminent serious damage to property. A record is made and kept of all uses of single separation in secure children's homes. Young people are offered the opportunity to read and add a permanent comment to the record of the separation.

23.14 There is an appropriate means for sending complaints or representations unopened to a designated complaints officer outside the establishment or to an advocate for the child.

23.15 The premises are fit for the purposes and are consistent with any Government guidance on this matter.

23.16 All staff working in secure children's homes are trained and competent to provide care in a secure environment.

23.17 Sentenced young persons in secure children's homes are supported by appropriately trained and experienced staff to confront and stop offending behaviour. Staff take specific measures to help to divert children and young people from future involvement in crime and anti-social behaviour.

23.18 Management of each unit is effective in, defines clear accountabilities for and regularly and frequently monitors the units care, safety, security, education and preparation for discharge and subsequent living in an open community.

Standard 24: Notification of Significant Events

Underpinning Legislation

Regulation 30: Notifiable events + Schedule 5

Outcome

All significant events relating to the protection of children accommodated in the home are notified by the registered person of the home to the appropriate authorities and appropriate action is taken following the incident

24.1 The registered person has a system in place to notify within 24 hours the persons and appropriate authorities of the occurrence of significant events in accordance with regulation 30. The system includes what to do where notifiable event arises at weekends.

24.2 A written record is kept which includes details of the action taken, and the outcome of any action or investigation, following a notifiable event.

24.3 The registered person has a system for notification to responsible authorities of any serious concerns about the emotional or mental health of a child such that a mental health assessment would be requested under the Mental Health Act 1983.

24.4 Following an incident notifiable under regulation 30, the home contacts the responsible authority to discuss any further action that may need to be taken.

Standard 25: Placement Plan & Review

Underpinning Legislation

Care Planning Regulations 2010

Outcome

Children are cared for in line with their individual Placement Plan/Short Break Care Plan

The home takes action to chase up outstanding reviews or visits from the responsible authority, contributes to those reviews and assists the child to contribute to their reviews

25.1 Children understand, within their level of understanding, the purpose and content of their plan and the reasoning behind any decisions about their care.

25.2 Each child's Placement Plan is monitored by a key worker within the home who ensures that the requirements of the plan are implemented in the day-to-day care of that child.

25.3 The home contributes effectively to each child's Placement Plan review and statutory review of the child's care plan. For children in a series of short breaks it will be the short break care plan which is reviewed.

25.4 The home assists the child to put forward their own current views, wishes and feelings in each review process, and helps to ensure that these are fully taken into account in each child's review.

25.5 The home contacts placing authorities to request statutory reviews or visits if overdue for any child, if a change in the care plan is needed, if there has been a significant change in arrangements for the child's care, or if a major action (e.g. a change of placement) not in the care plan appears likely, if the placing authority has not arranged the review.

25.6 The home ensures that if a child is not visited by their caseworker at the frequency expected by Regulations, or within a reasonable time following a reasonable request for a visit originated by the child, this is raised at the child's next review.

25.7 Children are assisted to secure the support of an independent advocate to support them in providing their views, wishes and feelings to statutory reviews.

25.8 The result of all statutory reviews and reviews of Placement Plans are recorded on the child's file, and individuals responsible for pursuing actions at the home arising from reviews are clearly identified

FEES & FREQUENCY OF INSPECTIONS

Her Majesty's Chief Inspector of Education, Children's Services & Skills (Fees & Frequency of Inspections (Children's Homes etc) Amendment Regulations 2010

- An application for registration by a person seeking to be registered as a person who carries on/provides the home:

  - £2,186.00

- An application for registration by a person who is seeking to be registered as a person who manages the home:

  - £596.00

- For an application in respect of a children's home for 3 or fewer residents:

  - By a person seeking to be registered as a person who provides it £596.00
  - By a person seeking to be registered as a person who manages it £ nil

Variation Fees

- Variation fee for application by registered provider under s.15(1)(a) CSA 2000 – (variation or removal of any condition for time being in force in relation to the registration):

- £1,093.40

■ For an application under s.15(1)(a) in respect of an establishment which is a 'small establishment', for an application by a person seeking to be registered as a person who carries on the establishment:

- Variation fee of £596.00

NB. In a case where the variation of a condition is a minor variation, the variation fee will be £99.00. A minor variation is one is one in which in the opinion of Ofsted, if the application for the variation were granted, would involve no material alteration in the register kept by it.

Annual Fees & Frequency of Inspection

■ The registered provider in respect of a children's home must pay an annual fee:

- For a children's home with 3 or fewer places a flat fee of £1093.40
- For a children's home with between 4 and 76 approved places,, the sum of £1093.40 + an amount of £108.90 for each approved place from the 4th to the 76th inclusive
- For a children's home that has more than 76 approved places, a flat fee of £9120.00

■ Children's Homes are subject to inspection at a minimum frequency of twice in every 12 month period. Any inspection may be unannounced.

Appendix: CAE Publications

Personal Guides from CAE Ltd Pantiles Langham Road
Robertsbridge East Sussex TN32 5EP tel: 01580 880243
email: *childact@caeuk.org* or order via our secure on-line
facility at *www.caeuk.org*

- Children Act 1989 in The Context of Human
  Rights Act 1998
- Children Act 2004
- Child Protection
- 'How Old Do I Have To Be?' (a simple guide
  to the rights and responsibilities of 0–21
  year olds)
- Sexual Offences Act 2003
- Children & Young Persons Act 2008
- Safeguarding Vulnerable Groups Act 2006
- Assessment of Special Educational Needs
- Criminal Justice & Immigration Act 2008
- Mental Capacity Act 2005
- Fostering
- Residential Care
- The Children (Scotland) Act 1995 in The
  Context of the Human Rights Act 1998

www.caeuk.org

Discounts on orders of 50 or more of any one title

Resource

Stockton

Riverside